Breathing Life
INTO SUNDAY SCHOOL

12 ESSENTIALS TO REVIVE YOUR MOST IMPORTANT MINISTRY

BY KEN BRADDY
foreword by Allan Taylor

© 2019 LifeWay Press • Reprinted March 2020

ISBN 9781535967211
Item 005817177

Ken Braddy
Manager of LifeWay's Adult Bible Study curriculum. Minister of Education
for twenty years. Adult Sunday School teacher. Blogger: KenBraddy.com.

Production Team
Team Leader/Editor: Brian Gass
Production Editor: Tessa Morrell
Graphic Designer: Lauren Rives

Groups Ministry
LifeWay Church Resources
One LifeWay Plaza
Nashville, TN 37234

By completing a study of this book, you can receive course credit in the
Christian Growth Study Plan. For more details, visit LifeWay.com/CGSP.

Dewey decimal classification: 268
Subject headings: SUNDAY SCHOOLS/RELIGIOUS EDUCATION

DEDICATION

To my mother, Millie, who loved me and took me to Sunday School.
And to my wife, Tammy, who has encouraged me as I've championed Sunday
School and its leaders. Thanks for sharing the journey with me.

TABLE of CONTENTS

Sunday School is about God's *day*. The first day of the week is when Jesus rose from the tomb. It's the day the early church observed to commemorate His bodily resurrection and has been the traditional practice of the New Testament church for two millennia.

Sunday School is about God's *house*. It's the place where we assemble together to worship our Lord and Savior. And it's the place where we gather in small group Bible studies to learn about: Why are we here? How did we get here? What's the purpose of being here? Where are we headed when life is over here?

Sunday School is about God's *Word*. The Bible is God's storybook for children, God's molding of youth, God's strength in young adulthood, God's ever-present help in middle age, and God's sustaining grace in old age.

Sunday School is about *people*. Preschoolers who need to be loved, children who need to learn, youth who need guidance, young adults who need truth, median adults who need challenging, and senior adults who need to end well.

Sunday School is about *transformation*. Heads that need renewing, hands that need to serve, feet that need to carry the gospel, hearts that need character, and souls that need saving.

Sunday School is about the *Great Commission*. Sunday School is how the church will evangelize, organize, mobilize, individualize, and energize so the Great Commission can be realized.

Sunday School is about *ministry*. Sunday School is a friend to the perishing, a hug to the hurting, a smile to the lonely, a support to the downcast, a prayer for the sick, and a comfort to the mourning.

Sunday School is about *inspiration*. Sunday School is a place to think something, a place to learn something, a place to feel something, and a place to do something.

This is the kind of Sunday School that my friend, Ken Braddy, will lead you to know, love, and implement in your church. Ken is a proven commodity. This man eats, sleeps, and breathes Sunday School. If truth were known, I bet he even dreams about Sunday School!

Ken has served churches as Minister of Education and as a Sunday School teacher. Although highly educated and intellectually brilliant, he is first and foremost a practitioner who has learned in the crucible of real life ministry. Every church Ken has served as Minister of Education has seen her Sunday School grow. One church grew from 44 to over 2,400! It is no stretch to call Ken a "Sunday School expert." The man knows his stuff. He has given his life to it!

He currently oversees LifeWay's four ongoing curriculum brands. That is no small task! In addition, he writes a daily Sunday School blog that is read by thousands of subscribers (kenbraddy.com) and speaks at numerous churches and Sunday School training events around the country. He has received several awards for his outstanding work in Sunday School.

Ken has been used of God to breathe life into many Sunday Schools and Sunday School leaders, and he will do the same for you.

Twelve is an important number in the Bible. Some theologians believe the number stands for totality and serves in establishing foundations. There are too many references to enumerate here, but consider these.

- God established the nation of Israel on the foundation of the twelve sons of Jacob who became the twelve tribes of Israel.
- Jesus established His church on the foundation of the twelve disciples whom He made apostles.
- Jesus established Himself as the "bread of life" on the foundation of feeding the 5,000 with twelve baskets of leftovers.
- God established the return of the Jews to Himself on the foundation of the 144,000 Jewish evangelists—12,000 from each of the twelve tribes during the Great Tribulation.

- God will establish the holy city, the New Jerusalem on twelve foundations.

Do you need to establish a new or strengthened Sunday School? *Breathing Life into Sunday School* details twelve ways that a church can experience new life and vibrancy in its Sunday School ministry. These twelve essentials are replicable by any church of any size and will serve as the foundation to build and strengthen your Bible study ministry. I believe if you follow these twelve Sunday School foundations you can experience the totality of your Sunday School ministry.

So, what are you waiting for? Get reading. Get implementing. Breathe life into your Sunday School!

Allan Taylor
Director, Sunday School & Church Education Ministry
LifeWay Christian Resources

MAN THE SHIP, AND BRING HER TO LIFE!

In 2001, the price of gas was only $1.46 per gallon.[1] *The Lord of the Rings* trilogy began,[2] as did Wikipedia.[3] Something else happened, too: 9/11. Terrorists flew airplanes into the World Trade Center's twin towers in New York City. Most of us can certainly remember where we were when we heard about that tragedy.

But something else happened in 2001 that may have escaped your notice. The United States Navy launched a new aircraft carrier. Named after one of our most popular presidents, the USS Ronald Reagan began its service that year.

When a ship is launched, it is done with a lot of fanfare. Mrs. Nancy Reagan, President Reagan's wife, was invited to speak at the ceremony. Thousands of sailors lined the deck of the massive aircraft carrier, standing at attention while Mrs. Reagan gave her speech. She concluded her tribute to her husband and signaled the beginning of the USS Ronald Reagan's service by uttering eight words that are spoken at ceremonies like this. As she ended her speech, she simply said, "Man the ship, and bring her to life." Thousands of sailors ran to their duty posts and assumed their stations. The massive aircraft carrier was brought to life as sailors eagerly ran to their assigned work stations. It was an unforgettable moment! The USS Ronald Reagan was for all practical purposes "dead in the water" until her crew brought the ship to life.[4]

Does your Sunday School feel a little like the USS Ronald Reagan before the speech? Does it have potential but need to be brought to life? If yes, then this book is for you. It has been created to encourage you to "man the ship [of Sunday School] and bring her to life." You can indeed breathe life into your Sunday School!

IT'S NOT QUITE DEAD

If almost 90% of all golfers used the same brand of golf ball, you'd probably conclude they know something about the quality and reliability of that particular kind of golf ball. If almost 90% of your friends dined regularly at a restaurant in your town, you'd rightly conclude they know a good thing when they experience it. If almost 90% of the automobiles on the road were created by one manufacturer, you'd probably be convinced everyone else knew something you didn't, and you might look to trade in your car for the brand they drive.

Then there is the issue of healthy, vibrant churches and the kind of Bible teaching strategies they implement for the people in their church and community. The church's mission is to make disciples. What if research demonstrates that almost 90% of vibrant churches use Sunday School as the ministry for delivering Bible teaching, making disciples, and for assimilating people into their churches? Would you be convinced that Sunday School might be worth considering? Would you stop listening to people who have declared that "Sunday School is dead"?

David Francis, former Director of Sunday School at LifeWay Christian Resources, conducted an analysis of the 400 vibrant churches that were surveyed for the book, *Simple Church*. He gathered data on 94% of the vibrant churches (a vibrant church was identified as one that had experienced at least 5% growth for three consecutive years). He discovered that 87.5% of those vibrant churches conducted Sunday School adjacent to the worship service on the Sunday morning schedule.[5]

Sunday School isn't dead. Yours may need new life breathed into it, but churches are succeeding in the ministry of Sunday School. When someone says, "Sunday School is dead," don't listen. But do listen to the heartbeat of your church's Sunday School. Do listen to what your members and guests say about it. If you believe it needs a good checkup, and perhaps needs some life breathed into it, this book is for you.

Maybe you've heard the phrase, "The grass is always greener on the other side." This kind of thinking has caused many churches to wonder whether or not Sunday School is still the right ministry for them. Tempted by the promises heard at a conference or those of an author, some church leaders have been tempted to abandon Sunday School and throw out the proverbial baby with the bath water when another option is presented.

In my experience, the grass isn't greener on the other side. The grass is always greener where it is watered. Sunday School can be a healthy, thriving ministry if we give it the time, attention, and resources it needs. Sunday School must be watered. Hear the words of David Francis, one of the champions of Sunday School. Here is what he says about the supposed death of Sunday School:

"Once in a while, you hear people say that Sunday School had its turn and it's time to move on to something new and innovative. I'm not against new and innovative. I think we should use the tools God gives us to reach the world for Christ. Internet conferencing, messaging, and smart phones all have their place. What disturbs me are the words *better* or *more effective* are usually left out of the discussion. When Sunday School is done right, it continues to be a proven and effective way of reaching the lost in our communities, involving the saved in service, and mobilizing the local church for ministry...I see it time and time again: Sunday School works and works well...if the leaders are willing to do the work. It is not easy, but nothing worth doing ever is."[6]

The other thing I'm convinced has happened is that some pastors and church leaders may never have been part of a church with a strong, vibrant Sunday School. In their experience, Sunday School doesn't work. I get that. I'm arguing for a revitalization of Sunday School. I'm saying that Sunday School can be a healthy ministry, but we must roll up our sleeves and go to work. I'm convinced that a Sunday School that isn't healthy can experience new life and vibrancy. People experience this all the time when they realize they are in poor health. Those people adopt new eating habits and exercise routines, and in time they lose weight, feel better, and have renewed energy. The same thing can happen with a church's Sunday School ministry. It can get healthier.

I am convinced that Sunday School works, but you must work Sunday School. It can be an effective ministry—a place where guests and members are assimilated into smaller disciple-making groups. Sunday School can build community, help people understand and apply the Bible, and give people a place to serve and use their God-given spiritual gifts. It doesn't have to just survive on life support.

MORE THAN JUST BIBLE STUDY

When I was in tenth grade, my Sunday School teacher was Mr. Cochran. He and his family owned a small fleet of airplanes and operated a flight school in my hometown. One Sunday afternoon a year, he'd take us boys up for a flight. It was the best day of the year.

I remember Mr. Cochran for an act of kindness he showed to me. At age sixteen, I wrecked my car at an intersection while making an unprotected left-hand turn. I'd just left the church-sponsored boys softball game in which I'd played. (Mr. Cochran doubled as the coach.) He was in the car behind mine and witnessed the accident that totaled my vehicle. I was thankful to walk away from the accident. I remember him asking me, "Do you want me to follow the wrecker to your house and speak to your father?" I eagerly answered in the affirmative. I don't remember a lot of what Mr. Cochran taught us, but I remember everything about this incident and how he went out of his way to help me. He loved me. I was one of his "Sunday School boys." He loved me in the classroom and out of the classroom. Sunday School was something he did 24/7. That's good Sunday School. It's more than just Bible study! Good Sunday School happens between Sundays. It's about relationships, fellowship, ministry, and serving others. It's about affecting every aspect of life.

I've had the privilege of leading three churches to grow and strengthen their Sunday School ministries. I've witnessed God-sized growth in one of those Sunday Schools. The first church I served—a small mission church—didn't stay small for long. On launch Sunday we had forty people in Sunday School. Ten years later when I transitioned to my second church, I left behind a Sunday School of over 2,400 members. God was truly at work there.

I've recently taught an adult group for six years as a lay leader, launching it as a "paper class." It grew, too, and my wife and I were blessed to welcome many new couples into our "empty nester" group. When I left this church where Tammy and I had been members, we left behind a wonderful group of adults and a healthy class we'd created. Today, they are still going strong.

At the time of the writing of this book, I'm serving part-time on a church staff in addition to my role at LifeWay Christian Resources. When I first became acquainted with this church, it had less than 200 people in Sunday School on an average Sunday. Today, after implementing some of the things you'll read about in this book, the church now has one of the fastest-growing Sunday Schools in Tennessee (percentage growth) year-over-year. The church has experienced new highs in Sunday School; we've started ongoing training for teachers; and we are exploring ways to provide more space to accommodate growth. We have a plan to reach an average attendance of 400 within the next twenty-four months. I believe we'll beat that goal.

I blog daily to encourage and equip Sunday School leaders. (You can subscribe for free at kenbraddy.com.) I've been encouraging and equipping pastors, directors, and teachers through the blog since 2011. Thousands of church leaders follow the blog daily, and I'd love for you to come and join this growing online community of teachers and leaders.

In every church I've served, I've seen Sunday School grow and improve its overall health. I've witnessed people sitting in circles, leaders guiding conversations, people ministering to one another, folks volunteering to serve inside the church, and people using their spiritual gifts to serve others outside the church. Of course, there were challenges along the way, and no church was perfect. But by and large, the Sunday Schools I've been part of have been healthy or experienced improved health. We discovered ways to breathe life into Sunday School. I want you to know how to do that, too.

WHAT ABOUT CHURCHES WITH OFF-CAMPUS GROUPS?

Churches that have chosen to implement a small group strategy for Bible study will also benefit from the contents in this book. So will churches that have adopted a hybrid approach to Bible study, offering both Sunday

School and small groups. The twelve essentials will apply to both of these types of churches.

SADDLE UP!

The Scripture says, "A horse is prepared for the day of battle, but victory comes from the LORD" (Prov. 21:31). I like this verse because it sums up an important truth. We must make preparation. Yes, we have to work to bring life back to the Sunday School, but we also must acknowledge that any victory we achieve ultimately comes from God. We never want to make a Sunday School turnaround seem like it was done because of our cunning, ingenuity, or hard work alone. We prepare for battle, but the victory comes from the Lord. So, to that end, we work hard, we pray, and we trust God for the results. Our job? Saddle the horse, do the hard work, be prepared, and ride into battle.

GETTING THE MOST OUT OF THIS BOOK

I've included practical insights along with suggestions for implementing the twelve essential principles. There are questions at the end of each chapter to help you process your thoughts. I'd encourage you to get a few copies and read it together with some friends and colleagues. There are others like you who care about your church's Bible teaching ministry, whatever you have chosen to call it. Sunday School, LIFE Groups, Community Groups are names for the groups in which your church gathers for Bible study, fellowship, and ministry.

I want to help you think through the twelve essential principles that have the potential to bring new health and strength to your Sunday School. These twelve principles will apply to churches of all sizes. Most of these won't take a lot of money. These twelve principles for breathing life into your Sunday School have been tried successfully, so I can recommend them to you with confidence.

Remember, Sunday School works, but you have to work Sunday School. So it's time to saddle up your Sunday School horse!

ESSENTIAL 1: TEACH WITH VARIETY

"We're not coming back to your church." That was the actual statement made to a pastor-friend of mine one Sunday. A guest family attended Sunday School at his small church on the northeast side of Dallas. After Sunday School, the family met with the congregation for worship at 11 a.m. Pastor Ron saw the family sitting among the regular attenders and determined to greet them after the service. Pastor Ron enthusiastically thanked them for being guests that day and asked whether or not they might want to grab lunch the following Sunday. That's when the father told him, "We're not coming back."

The man went on to explain to Pastor Ron that he and his wife had a less than stellar experience in Sunday School. An unprepared group leader sat behind a small table and read the Bible study lesson to the group. Interaction was minimal. The teaching wasn't done with excellence or variety. The lesson was boring. Before this family ever made it to the worship service, their experience in Sunday School had convinced them to look elsewhere for a church home. The pastor is my brother-in-law.

This real-life example has caused me to wonder how many times it is repeated elsewhere on Sunday mornings. It drives home the fact that teaching matters. Teachers have such a profound influence on people through their Bible teaching ministries. Unfortunately for the church, only a small percentage of teachers communicate with excellence and utilize a variety of teaching methods. In my experience, most teachers use one or two primary methods they prefer. Those methods are like their favorite pair of jeans—comfortable and familiar. The problem? Not everyone in their group likes those methods as much as the group leader does.

TEACHING IS MORE THAN TELLING

It's unfortunate when teachers believe their job is to provide "an information dump" for their group members. Biblical information is needed, but teaching is more than just presenting facts. Christian educator Dr. Rick Yount has spent a lifetime studying and teaching how people learn. Dr. Yount, in speaking about brain research and how people learn, says, "It compels me to keep fighting the pervasive idea that teaching is simply telling what you know. Teaching, discipling, and equipping find their power in the consistent and persistent focusing of the learners' minds on biblical concepts and conceptual relationships, spiritual attitudes and priorities, and ministry skills...with the intent of changing each learner for the better. Teaching is creating a learning environment that evokes, energizes, and maintains student attention on the truths, values, and skills of God's kingdom—indeed, on God Himself—that will transform them. We eventually become—head, heart, and hand—what we attend to."[7] As you can see, making disciples is more than just telling them information. It's about engaging them in a holistic teaching-learning process.

GOD'S COMMUNICATION STYLE

God the Father communicated in a variety of ways during the time of the Old Testament. Hebrews 1:1-2 says, "Long ago God spoke to the fathers by the prophets at different times and in different ways. In these last days, he has spoken to us by his Son" (Heb. 1:1-2). Some translations read, "various ways" or "diverse ways." At any rate, the emphasis is on variety.

Years ago, I was exposed to the teaching of Dr. Howard Hendricks. In a video series by Walk Thru the Bible Ministries designed to train teachers, Dr. Hendricks argued for variety in the classroom. He was passionate about the need for teachers to vary the way they taught the Bible. In that video series, Dr. Hendricks explained that when God had content to communicate to his "class" (a person or a people group), He used a variety of methods. In no particular order, he reminded the audience of the following ways that God communicated to man in the Old Testament. The following examples demonstrate the qualities of God's various communication styles:

1. **Visual.** God frequently communicated visually through such things as the rainbow, or the pillars of fire and smoke. The bloody sacrifices performed by priests were visual reminders of the seriousness of sin.

2. **Unexpected.** Balaam's donkey is a good example of something that was totally unexpected. Moses' burning bush would also qualify as an unexpected type of communication. When God communicated, it was often a surprise.

3. **Multi-sensory.** The Egyptian plagues created havoc for that nation. The people handled dead frogs, picking them up and throwing them into fires to dispose of them. Not only did they touch them, but they also saw and smelled the frogs.

4. **Unique.** How often did a donkey talk? Once. How many times did angels sing to announce the birth of someone? Only once. When God used a method of communication once, He sometimes never repeated it again. That's just the opposite of the way you and I would communicate!

5. **Memorable.** When God communicated, it was always unforgettable. The parting of the Red Sea was memorable. The burning bush was memorable. Do the members of our groups remember a thing we've said after we've taught a Bible study? Just how memorable are they?

6. **Captivating.** This word comes from a Latin word meaning "to capture." It has the idea that a person's attention is quick to run away and that the teacher must continually snare and capture the attention of group members. The handwriting on the wall in Daniel 5 is an example of how God communicated and captured the attention of everyone at a banquet.

7. **Incarnational.** As Hebrews 1:2 reminds us, God has spoken to us in these final days through His Son. Jesus lived among us and communicated things from His Father to us in fresh ways never before seen.[8]

The good news for group leaders is that they can emulate all seven styles of communication used by God the Father. It just takes some time and forethought as to how one or two might be used in a teaching session.

HOW DID JESUS COMMUNICATE?

When Jesus appeared and began His public ministry, He continued His Father's style of communication; Jesus taught in a variety of ways. This is very different than the way you and I often teach. We tend to find a method or two we like, and we use them most of the time. The people in our groups can anticipate exactly what we'll do every time our Bible study group comes together to study the Bible. In fact, they can do this with a high degree of accuracy.

This is not the way Jesus taught. He was the Master Teacher. He could teach anywhere—in a home, on the side of a road, at a temple or synagogue, from a boat, on a hillside, and a myriad other places. He could also teach in many different ways. Although He did not have the technological advances we have today, He was able to communicate His messages with an amazing array of teaching methods. We know of at least 20 or more ways that Jesus communicated:

- Object lessons (John 4:1-42)
- Points of contact (John 1:35-51)
- Problem-solving (Mark 10:17-22)
- Conversation (Mark 10:27)
- Questions (As recorded in the Gospels, Jesus asked over 100 questions to provoke people to think and seek the truth.)
- Answers (Jesus used His answers to move people from where they were to where they needed to be in order to grow spiritually. Jesus encouraged people to discover the truth.)
- Lecture (Matt. 5–7; John 14–17)
- Parables (John 10:1-21; 15:1-10)
- Scripture (Jesus quoted extensively from the Old Testament when teaching.)
- Teachable moments (John 4:5-26)
- Contrast (Matt. 5:21-22,33-34,38-39)
- Concrete and literal examples (Matt. 6:26-34)
- Symbols (Matt. 26:17-20)
- Large and small groups (Matt. 5–7; John 14–17)

- Individual teaching opportunities (John 3:1-21)
- Modeling (Matt. 15:32)
- Motivation (Matt. 16:24-27)
- Impression and expression (Matt. 4:19-20; 7:20)
- Himself (Matt. 28:19-20)[9]

If you are a group leader, how many of the preceding teaching methods have you used with your group in the past month? The last 90 days? The last six months? I don't want to discourage you, but most of us don't vary our teaching methods as much as we should. The challenging thing is that the above list isn't an exhaustive list. Jesus used other methods besides the ones listed here. He set a great example, though, of what can be done when we plan and use our God-given abilities to more effectively communicate the Scriptures.

A skilled baseball pitcher can place his fingers on a baseball and alter the way it performs as it is hurled toward home plate. No pitcher would dare throw the same pitch at a batter over and over again. Nor would a football team run the same two or three plays throughout a game. The opposing team would be able to anticipate and stop the offense with little or no problem.

Think about the members of your Bible study group. Maybe you are a member. Perhaps you are the group leader. Can you anticipate what is going to take place the next time your group meets? Can you list the actions that will be taken and the order in which they will occur? Can you also put a time estimate next to each activity? You and I both know the answer is "yes." Most members of a Bible study group can anticipate what is going to happen down to the minute. There are no surprises. Things are too repetitive. The group's study time has become stale. If the members of a Bible study group are "reading the coach's playbook," it's time to throw out that playbook and introduce a changeup. It's time to run a new play. It's time to teach with some variety. Experts have declared "Each lesson needs to involve a variety of learning activities…"[10] One of my heroes in Christian education once said, "Maximum learning happens when there is maximum involvement."[11]

People who have dedicated their lives to helping group leaders become better communicators recognize the need to teach with variety.

IN A SENSE

I like the way John Milton Gregory put it when he wrote about the importance of teaching in such a way that appeals to our five senses. He said, "each sense organ is a gateway to the mind of the pupil...the mind attends to that which makes a powerful appeal to the senses."[12] Today, we continue to discover how communication styles that appeal to a variety of senses are needed. TED Talks have become very popular. Delivered in eighteen minutes or less, presentations made by the most effective TED Talks presenters engage the senses of their audience members. "The bottom line is this: people remember information more vividly when more than one sense is stimulated."[13] Because appealing to the five senses creates a better learning experience for everyone in a Bible study group, here are a few ways to use the five senses to communicate biblical content:

1. **Seeing:** display a map, call attention to a poster, bring an object, use a slideshow presentation, use wall-size sticky notes and ask group members to respond to assignments written on them, play a video clip

2. **Hearing:** create listening teams, play music, listen to a recording

3. **Smelling:** introduce scents such as lavender, peppermint, and rosemary; bake some goodies to share with the group

4. **Touching:** give group members a handout or a fill-in-the-blank sheet, pass around an object from an object lesson, pray and hold hands

5. **Tasting:** sample food and drinks that connect to your Bible study such as bread, juice, roasted foods, etc.

THE DIFFERENT WAYS PEOPLE LEARN

"The theory of multiple intelligences challenges old beliefs about what it means to be smart...Our culture has focused too much attention on verbal and logical thinking—the abilities typically assessed on an intelligence test—and neglected other ways of knowing...[Research has demonstrated] there are at least seven intelligences worthy of being taken seriously as important modes of thought."[14] These intelligences are ways that people take in information and process it; some people have called these "preferred learning styles."

We all learn in different ways, and according to the theory of multiple intelligences, we're all smart. The way I prefer to learn may not be the same way you do, but that doesn't minimize me or my learning preferences; they are just different than yours. That's why variety is so important in a Bible study. How boring would a Bible study be in which the group leader only used one or two primary methods of communicating content? It happens almost every time a group gathers for Bible study. Teachers default to what is comfortable for them; they default to their preferred learning style or styles. To be more effective as communicators of God's Word, we must realize that people learn in a variety of ways, and that requires us to teach in a variety of ways. Here are the seven intelligences defined in the book, *7 Kinds of Smart* by Thomas A. Armstrong. Which two most describe who you are and how you prefer to learn?

1. **Linguistic Intelligence.** The intelligence of words. This is the intelligence of the storyteller, journalist, poet, and lawyer. People who are particularly smart in this area can argue, persuade, entertain, or instruct effectively through the spoken word.

2. **Logical-mathematical Intelligence.** The intelligence of numbers and logic. This is the intelligence of scientists, accountants, and computer programmers. These people are able to reason, sequence, see cause-and-effect, find numerical patterns, and create hypotheses.

3. **Spatial Intelligence.** This intelligence involves thinking in pictures and images. It is the ability to perceive, transform, and recreate different aspects of the visual-spatial world. It's the playground of architects, photographers, artists, pilots, and mechanical engineers.

4. **Musical Intelligence.** People with this intelligence appreciate rhythms and melodies. It's the intelligence of a Bach, Beethoven, or Brahms. Yet musical intelligence resides in the mind of any individual who has a good ear, can sing a tune, or keep time to music.

5. **Bodily-kinesthetic Intelligence.** Persons with this intelligence are talented at controlling their body movements and can handle objects

skillfully. Athletes, craftsmen, mechanics, and surgeons possess a great measure of this kind of thinking.

6. **Interpersonal Intelligence.** This is the ability to understand and work with people. People with this intelligence are responsive to people's temperaments, intentions, and desires. These people are able to get inside the skin of someone else and see their point of view. They make wonderful networkers, teachers, and negotiators.

7. **Intrapersonal Intelligence.** This is the intelligence of the inner self. Persons with this intelligence are able to access their own feelings, and they can discriminate between many different kinds of inner emotional states. They can enjoy meditation and contemplation, deep soul-searching, and can be very self-disciplined. Counselors, theologians, and self-employed business people often have this intelligence.[15]

If you are a group leader, there's a very good chance that two of these intelligences have become your primary way to teach your Bible study each week. The company I work for has taken these seven intelligences and changed the nomenclature slightly. I think our version is easier to remember! We've even added an eighth one—Natural—to help group leaders understand how people in their groups prefer to learn by connecting with nature or objects from nature. In conference settings and training venues, I frequently teach people these eight learning approaches:

1. Relational
2. Reflective
3. Visual
4. Verbal
5. Musical
6. Physical
7. Logical
8. Natural

What is the implication for groups and group leaders? Plenty. Each of the groups in our churches have people in them who have a preferred way of learning. Group members may prefer to learn in ways the teacher does not. As a teacher-leader, I cannot afford to teach in one or two ways that I prefer. I must use a variety of learning approaches to make sure I am communicating effectively with people in my group who learn differently than I do. The people in my group are smart, but in ways that are different from me.

7 THINGS YOU SHOULD KNOW ABOUT TEACHING METHODS

I was first introduced to LeRoy Ford's work when I was in seminary. His books on Christian education and teaching were required reading, and thankfully I've held onto his books over the years. I'm glad they are in my personal library, and I'm delighted to share his thoughts about teaching methods. To breathe life into Sunday School, teachers can help by varying their methods, but they should remember:

1. No method is of itself effective or ineffective. It all depends upon what we do with it.

2. The method depends upon the ability of the teacher. Improvement will come in time and with practice.

3. The method chosen depends upon the abilities of the learner. Some methods are more appropriate for one group rather than another. Know your group.

4. The method depends upon the size of the group. Some teaching methods are better for smaller groups and vice-versa.

5. The method depends upon the time available. A group activity will take longer than one executed only by the group leader (because he or she is in control of the time).

6. If you use methods that involve groups within the group, just remember that things often take longer than you think they will.

7. The method depends upon the facilities. The room you teach in can help or hinder the methods you choose. Choose wisely![16]

AN IDEAL SUNDAY SCHOOL SESSION

What I am about to describe may not typically take place in your Bible study group at present. But what if it did? What if you changed a few things about the way you teach? What if you began appealing to people's preferred learning styles? A typical day in your Bible study group might look something like this.

- You arrive early and set up a small portable speaker that connects wirelessly to your smart phone. You begin playing a song that is looped to repeat until you end it. The music is playing in the background and relates to your Bible study in some way.
- You place an index card on each chair and write instructions on the marker board, telling group members to answer a question on their card in response to the question you've written on the marker board.
- You welcome guests, make announcements, and pray. The Bible study continues.
- You ask each person to read one verse of the long passage that you are studying. Person one reads the first verse, person two reads the second verse, and so on.
- You ask a discussion question and give group members time to respond.
- After giving the group a mini-lecture on a particular part of the lesson passage, you ask group members to divide into smaller groups of three or four (triads or quads) and respond to a reflective question you pose to them.
- You continue to study the Scripture passage, directing the group's attention to a poster or map on the wall as you explain the significance of a location or a person mentioned in the passage.
- You remind the group members of the song they heard while they arrived for the Bible study, and you ask them to connect the words of the song to the topic you are studying.
- You suggest three ways to apply the lesson to life.
- You pray and dismiss the group.

If this sounds like a normal group experience, that's great! If not, let's think back through this scenario and see how many learning styles were used.

1. **Reflective:** the group leader asked a reflective question.
2. **Musical:** a song was used to set the mood and to generate discussion.
3. **Physical:** group members filled out a response on an index card.
4. **Visual:** group members saw a map or poster, and instructions were written on a marker board.
5. **Relational:** group members answered a question in triads/quads.
6. **Verbal:** group members responded to questions.
7. **Logical:** group members saw a place on a map or a list of information about a person on a poster; they also saw or heard a list of three ways to apply the study.

It was not hard to use all seven learning approaches in this one Bible study! And it didn't feel "Frankenstein-ish." Everything flowed well and worked together to create an interactive, dynamic experience. But here is what typically happens:

1. A group leader opens the study in prayer.
2. The group leader or a group member reads the passage of Scripture being studied.
3. The group leader asks a few questions (not really great discussion questions, just questions).
4. The group leader makes some comments about the passage from some notes he's put together from his study time.
5. Someone prays and ends the group's study.

In the above example, only a few learning approaches are used, not seven or eight. For the most part, the lesson appealed to verbal learners. Missing were the visual and relational elements in the first teaching scenario. Musically-inclined learners were left out, too. Visual learners didn't have much to excite them. No wonder people leave a class with a "ho hum" experience. No wonder Sunday School struggles to grow and be healthy.

If you want to breathe life into Sunday School, you must have a Sunday School in which the teachers know, understand, and utilize the multiple learning approaches described in this chapter.

FOR FURTHER THOUGHT

1. What is your preferred learning style? How has God wired you to take in information?

2. When is the last time you experienced a teaching session that appealed to your top preferred learning approaches? What was so appealing about the way the teacher led the Bible study?

3. How could you introduce the group leaders at your church to the concepts in this chapter?

4. Does the curriculum used by your group leaders (if they use a curriculum from a Christian publisher) intentionally incorporate the eight learning approaches? How many do they typically incorporate?

ESSENTIAL 2: FEED IT FINANCIALLY

Several years ago, my wife and I began watching home improvement shows on cable television. They were quite addictive! Those shows inspired us to begin some remodeling projects at our house. Before we remodeled one thing in the house, we changed our budget. We moved money around so that we would have funds for the projects we wanted to undertake. One year we budgeted to have the carpet removed from our downstairs floors, replacing it with hardwood instead. The next year we budgeted to have our master bathroom upgraded. Today, upgrades continue.

If you want to know what a priority is to someone, follow the money trail. Priorities always receive a significant part of the budget. The budget always tells you what's important to an individual, a family, a business, or a church. What would the money trail tell me about the importance of Sunday School to your church?

FEEDING AND GROWING GO HAND-IN-HAND

I have a new grandson. Logan James Braddy came into the world in October 2017. His parents learned very quickly that he likes to eat. In fact, from the day we first saw him, to the second time we saw him a month later, he'd grown significantly. Healthy things grow. Growing things must be fed.

Every once in a while, the evening news carries a story about people who are starving somewhere in the world. Occasionally stories hit closer to home, and we hear a local special interest story about pets that have been deprived of food and water by their owners; they are found starving but are often rescued and restored to health. These kinds of stories trigger our emotions. We react. Sometimes we overreact. We want to get involved. We want to make a difference.

Do we feel the same strong emotions for the Sunday School when it is hungry, perhaps even starving? A friend once said, "If you starve anything long enough, it will die." These words rang with truth. Let's change the phrase up a bit and see if it works in the context of the local church. "If you starve the Sunday School long enough, it will die." True or false?

The Sunday Schools of many churches are starving. They have life but are becoming weaker. The Sunday School still has a heartbeat, but it's faint. The process of decline is so slow, it's practically imperceptible. The Sunday School appears to have life, but it's slowly being starved. It isn't receiving enough financial nourishment to thrive.

2009 AND THE GREAT RECESSION

When the Great Recession began, I missed the early warning signs. At that time, I lived in the Dallas-Fort Worth metroplex. The local economy was more insulated from the effects of the recession at first, so I didn't notice the handwriting on the wall.

I changed jobs in 2010, and we moved out of state. We put our house up for sale, not fully appreciating the changes taking place around us in the economy. I thought selling the house would be a relatively quick and easy task. Our family lived on a cul-de-sac. There were two banana trees in the backyard. We lived just minutes from the Dallas-Fort Worth airport. I was sure the house would sell in just a few days.

Unfortunately, it took almost a year to sell that house. At one point we ended up with two house payments. A thief stole our pool equipment after my family moved out. My family and I made financial adjustments.

My family felt the effects of the recession. Then I began noticing the effects of the recession in the local church. I heard stories of long-tenured staff leaders whose jobs were deleted. Colleagues found themselves in dire straits. Church budgets were cut back and certain tasks once paid for by the church were taken over by volunteer members to save money.

The church experienced a new reality. Offerings declined as families scrambled to hold onto their houses. Two-income families often became single-income homes as layoffs occurred. We all learned to do more with less. We learned how to stretch budgets. And so did the church. The church tightened its financial belt. Sunday School felt the trickle-down effects.

UNHEALTHY ADJUSTMENTS

Once personnel cutbacks were made, churches continued to look for ways to make ends meet. Next on the chopping block? Bible study curriculum. I understand the decision. It even makes sense on the surface. Eliminate the expensive "quarterlies" that people have used for years and save the church some money. Encourage group leaders to teach the Bible from the Bible. Who needs curriculum? This began one of the most hurtful trends in the church; it continues today in some places.

A JUDGES 21:25 SUNDAY SCHOOL

The difficult year I had selling my house pales in comparison to the difficult year my family experienced as we searched for a new church home. Locating a church to visit wasn't the problem. There were plenty of those—practically one on every corner. The problem I had was finding a church that actually budgeted to provide Bible study curriculum for its group members. We visited a half-dozen churches of varying sizes. Only one provided curriculum for group members. One.

My wife and I visited one particular church in our new hometown. We visited several of the adult Bible study groups. None of them used an ongoing Bible study curriculum.

One group leader strolled into the classroom one Sunday morning. This group leader dropped his Bible and belongings onto his wooden podium with a resounding thud. He ran his fingers through his hair, looked at the group, and said, "Hey, I didn't have time to write a lesson this week because we attended three graduation parties, so take out your Bibles and turn to, oh, Proverbs 1."

We sat there in shock. Was this a joke?

The teacher asked a group member to read a few verses of Proverbs 1. When he finished reading, the group leader asked, "So, what do these verses mean to you?" He took a sip of his coffee while we tried to process what had just happened. I sat there in amazement.

My wife and I continued to visit groups in that church's teaching ministry, hoping to connect with one that used some type of ongoing curriculum. We couldn't find one. Group leaders wrote studies and were allowed to teach on any topic they wanted. Most of the studies were not good. The teachers meant well, but they lacked the skills to produce engaging Bible studies.

You might be asking yourself, "So what's the big deal about providing or not providing Bible study resources to Sunday School members and guests? Why not just let group leaders teach the Bible from the Bible?"

I can think of several reasons why budgeting for curriculum is an effective, long-term strategy for a church; curriculum is worthy of the church's financial investment. I say this from the vantage point of a group leader. I also say this from the vantage point of someone who has over twenty years of experience growing and leading Sunday Schools as an education/discipleship pastor.

1. **Curriculum creates balance.** Most group leaders have topics or books of the Bible they really like. If they aren't careful, group leaders will create imbalanced teaching plans that cause them to linger too long in either the Old or New Testament. They'll hover over a pet theological topic or a favorite book. Some will even take one or two verses of Scripture a week and major on minutia. Group members are inadvertently deprived of "the entire counsel of God" when any of these things take place. Curriculum, however, is based on a scope and sequence. The scope is the group of topics that can be covered. The sequence is the order in which those topics are covered. The development of a sound scope and sequence requires many hours to prepare but ultimately provides a well-balanced approach for studying the Bible.

2. **Group leaders are busy people.** Most group leaders are volunteer leaders. That means they have full- or part-time jobs. Some are raising children. Others are caring for aging parents. Some are climbing the corporate ladder. Still others are involved in multiple ministries at the church. The average group leader just doesn't have the time or energy to create outstanding studies each week. It's too much to expect them to do this. Group leaders should spend their time discipling people and ministering to their group members and guests, rather than spending hours of time writing weekly Bible studies.

3. People no longer attend every week. If you haven't noticed, attendance patterns have changed. Today, group members might attend once or twice a month, considering themselves to be very committed. Work, travel, kids sporting events, aging parents, the desire for leisure time all contribute to people's irregular attendance. What are those people to do while they are away from their Bible study group? If Bible study resources are provided by the church for group members, they can read, respond, and pray as they keep up with their group. Dr. Brad Waggoner conducted research on the factors that were common in people who grew spiritually year over year. The results were published in his book *The Shape of Faith to Come*. His discovery? The number one predictor of year-over-year spiritual growth was a person's daily engagement in reading the Bible.[17] It's important for group members to learn to self-feed daily, and curriculum makes this easier.

4. Group leaders are not trained theologians. Church leaders are told to guard the doctrine of the church closely (1 Tim. 4:16), and group leaders are on the front lines of teaching the members of our churches. Limited by time, these group leaders are also limited in their training in Scripture. Few hold advanced degrees in theology, Christian education, archaeology, or church history. Companies that produce curriculum have teams of people with theological and education degrees who design and create trustworthy resources.

5. You're investing in people's growth and discipleship. I've heard church leaders say, "The cost of curriculum is just too high! We can't afford it." I'd like to turn that on its head and say, "You can't afford not to provide your people with curriculum!" Personal Study Guides created by a Christian publisher might cost between $3-4 per person. But they contain thirteen studies, which means they average only $.04 per day per person! What other resource can the church provide that is crafted with purpose and created by people who are experts for under a nickel a day? None I'm aware of.

6. Personal Study Guides can be used to increase participation in the group Bible study. A savvy group leader will use the Personal Study Guide to involve group members in the Bible study session.

Asking people to read sections, respond to questions, fill in blanks, take notes, and jot down prayer requests in the Personal Study Guide are just a few ways to make this Bible study tool a valuable part of the group Bible study experience.

7. **New group leaders are more easily recruited when you provide curriculum.** David Francis was LifeWay's Director of Sunday School for over a decade. He's a good friend, an expert in Sunday School, and someone I deeply respect. Here's what David said in a book he recently authored. Regarding curriculum, new group leaders, and Sunday School, David maintains, "The choice of curriculum is important not only for ongoing Bible study but also in the enlistment and training of teachers and leaders. We do not want a person who is sitting in an adult class observing the teacher to think, 'I could never do that.' Rather, we want them to think, 'I could do that if they gave me the same resources.' The trend toward allowing adult teachers to 'do their own thing' is reversing. Today many growing churches are asking adult teachers to use the same curriculum or limiting their choices of curriculum. It's incredibly more efficient to enlist and train new leaders if all leaders are using similar curriculum. It's easier to supply support resources. It's easier to enlist and equip substitutes—who are potential future apprentices."[18]

Why would a church cut back on its curriculum budget when there are so many benefits for group leaders and group members? Short term financial gains may be possible, but long-term losses are inevitable. The Lord commissioned His church to go and make disciples. We are instructed to teach them to obey all He commanded (Matt. 28:18-20). Budgeting for curriculum is one way a church expresses obedience to the Great Commission. Starve anything long enough and it will die.

A LESSON LEARNED

I had trouble selling my home in Texas in 2010. There was an excess of houses in inventory. The recession was full-on. During this time, I learned a great lesson from a real estate agent. It's a lesson that churches can benefit from, too.

When we listed our house for sale, a realtor friend, a man named Scott and a member of our church, walked through our house and measured each room. He needed that information for the MLS (Multiple Listing Service). He wanted to help us sell our house.

After two months on the market, Scott came to my house one night and had a difficult conversation with my wife and I. He explained why our house wasn't getting any offers. He looked at us and said, "Your house is too cluttered to sell. The walls need a new coat of paint. Your kitchen is outdated." The feedback from potential buyers was hard to hear.

"What do you mean outdated?" we asked.

Scott proceeded to point out multiple things that made our house less desirable to buyers. He encouraged us to place several pieces of larger furniture in storage. He asked us to consider thinning out our closets. He recommended a painter.

How had we missed all of this? Wasn't it apparent that these things needed to be done?

The answer was "no." It wasn't apparent to us because we lived in the house and saw these things daily. We were so familiar with our home that we quit noticing the little things that buyers saw right away.

Tammy and I adjusted our budget to address Scott's concerns. We did as he suggested. We re-allocated funds to have items placed in storage. We thinned out closets. We did some remodeling in the kitchen. We painted the walls in neutral colors. And it finally paid off when we got multiple offers. In fact, two potential buyers bid each other up.

THE FOREST FOR THE TREES

I've visited churches and seen classrooms that need to lose a piano that has been donated by well-meaning people. Student ministries often take lots of donated furniture, too. There are countless classrooms that need a fresh coat of paint, or age-appropriate toys for the children; other rooms have been turned into storage rooms. Haven't you been in classrooms where several styles of chairs have been used? Over time we quit seeing these things. I've actually taught in a room with a giant coffee stain in the middle of the floor.

My friend Allan Taylor has had similar experiences. He said, "When I go to other churches to speak, it is always interesting to me to walk through the church's educational facilities. Many times, it is obvious they are not expecting company. The rooms are cluttered and unkept. There is a piano in the corner of the room with all kinds of hymnals, books, and other literature stacked on top of it...I told them Jesus died for people, not furniture. Make room for the people, and get rid of those old couches that some flea-bitten dog had laid on before they were generously donated to the church."[19]

Although our members are used to seeing the clutter, I wonder what guests think when they visit a group? It's probably nothing good. Be honest about your church for a moment. What needs some attention right now? Where could you direct finances in order to clean, update, or renovate your church's education space? We must feed the Sunday School financially.

We've often grown so accustomed to seeing the clutter in our churches that we fail to budget and fix the problems that guests see the minute they walk through the doors of the church. Look at your church's Sunday School budget. Will you find money for Bible study materials? Building improvements? New technology? Improved signage? Upgraded carpet, additional chairs, and so on? If you want to breathe life into Sunday School, you must feed it financially. Starve anything long enough and it will die.

FOR FURTHER THOUGHT

1. Is your Sunday School starving financially, or is it well-fed? What evidence do you see of this? Look back at several years of budgets to determine if the funds are increasing, decreasing, or about the same.

2. If you had an infusion of new monies that could be devoted to Sunday School, how would you spend them? Make a wish list.

3. Force-rank the items you listed in #2 above. Which project should be tackled first? Second? Third?

4. How does your church view curriculum? Is it seen as an investment in people's discipleship, or is it looked upon as an expense? How could you begin to change people's mindset so they value it more highly?

03

ESSENTIAL 3: GIVE IT ATTENTION

I recently got some unsettling news.

My company sponsored a free health screening, and I decided to take advantage of the convenience. I fasted for over twelve hours before having lab work done to determine my overall physical state. I met with a nurse who drew blood, checked my height and weight, and ran other tests. Then I received the results.

Talk about a wakeup call. I have neglected going to a doctor for regular checkups. My wife has encouraged me to get an annual physical for some time now. I've resisted. But now, after having my attention focused on the results of the lab work, I'm determined to do something about it. I've already begun changing eating and exercise habits.

I realized that focusing attention on my health brought me to a point of decision. I read my health report and decided to act. If my attention hadn't focused on my current physical state, I'd still be doing business as usual. Not anymore.

Think about your Sunday School. Whatever it is today, it is the result of decisions made in the past. My current physical state is the result of the decisions I've made in the past. Sunday School is the result of decisions made in the past, too.

If you want to breathe life into Sunday School, you must give it attention. Attention leads to awareness. Awareness leads to action.

FOCUS ATTENTION THROUGH THE NEW MEMBERS CLASS

I've served on three church staffs. The first church I served was a new, small mission church. We were blessed to see God work in our midst. The Sunday School became the fastest growing Sunday School in my state. We held onto that honor for several years. The Sunday School grew exponentially. More on that later.

The second church I served was very different. It was over 50 years old. It was traditional. Sunday School growth had stalled. Training was nonexistent. The Sunday School had flat-lined. It was in trouble. The pastor and I worked to create a class for potential new members where none existed before. He promoted it to the congregation, and invitations to attend were sent from his office to every guest. People responded.

The class was conducted every other month. I taught it on Sunday mornings while my pastor preached two worship services. He and the rest of the church staff joined us at noon for a lunch, and then he led the campus tour before the group dismissed.

One of the things emphasized during the new members class was the importance of belonging to a Bible study group. We provided participants with a list of groups. We talked about their options and how excited our groups would be if our guests visited them.

Much to our surprise, something wonderful took place. Sunday School attendance began to rise. And rise. And it rose some more. These potential new members did what we suggested. They were eager to take the next step. We simply told them what to do in order to have a deeper connection and a better experience at the church.

As we began doing some investigation of our own, we discovered that about 80% of the people who attended the new members class committed to belong to one of the church's adult Bible study groups. We were thrilled! Every other month we called attention to the Sunday School in this class.

We continued to realize growth in part because we focused attention on the Sunday School. We told the potential new members exactly what we wanted them to do. "Attend worship, join a group, find a ministry." We discovered a secret: focusing attention on Sunday School was a good thing. People wanted to know what their next step should be. We simply focused their attention on belonging to a Sunday School group. They responded.

We hadn't focused enough attention on the Sunday School with our potential new members until we started doing so at the new members class. Once we told them our expectations, they responded. Once we focused attention on group membership, they said yes. Why hadn't we focused attention on this before? We had just assumed that people knew the next step to take. They didn't.

FOCUS ATTENTION ON SUNDAY SCHOOL ANNUALLY

Most churches re-launch their Sunday School ministry in August around back-to-school time. Kids and students promote to the next grade level, just like they do as they go back to public school. Promotion Sunday (or Back-To-School Sunday as some like to call it) is a perfect occasion to focus your church's attention on the importance of Sunday School. In fact, the entire month of August is a good time to focus on Sunday School.

There are some important things churches can do to capitalize on this important time of the year. Focus the congregation's attention on the need to be involved in a Bible study group by doing any of the following:

1. **Preach a message about the importance of teaching God's Word.** A pastor's message is especially important around Promotion Sunday. It is a great day to remind people of the importance of teaching God's Word. It's a time to challenge the members to serve as group leaders and apprentice teachers in all age groups. By now the current year's teachers have been recruited, but it's good to plant seeds for next year.

2. **Recognize Sunday School teachers in the church's worship service.** Asking teachers to stand or calling them to the front of the worship center where they can be prayed for is a way to remind the congregation that the church's Bible teaching ministry requires many dedicated workers who give selflessly of their time.

3. **Pray for group leaders and directors.** Ask the congregation to pray for group leaders and those who direct the church's age group education ministries. This could be done in the worship service.

4. **Invite group members to share stories from the platform.** Enlist a few group members to briefly share why they value their Bible study group. These group members will call attention to things they appreciate such as quality Bible teaching, relationships with fellow group members, the ministry they do together as a group, the benefits of sharing life together, and so on.

5. **Have an enrollment emphasis in the worship service.** Challenge guests and unconnected members to fill out an expression of interest card that you've placed in the worship guide. Use the information to get people connected to groups before Promotion Sunday.

6. **Ask group leaders to contact absentees.** In anticipation of Promotion Sunday, it would be very appropriate for group leaders to contact absentees to remind them about taking part in Promotion Sunday. It is information they need to know, and they also need to know they are missed and that someone cares about them.

7. **Have a focused time of training.** Promotion Sunday is a good time around which to schedule an annual training event for the church's Bible study leaders. It's a smart way to kick off the new year of Bible study, and you can share enrollment and attendance goals, and cast vision for the church's Bible teaching ministry.

8. **Advertise your post-Labor Day Bible studies.** Tell people about the Bible studies that will take place in September. Invite them to connect with a group.

9. **Update the church's print and digital media.** As Promotion Sunday approaches, update any printed brochures you give to guests. Accurately list teachers and classrooms, and then use that information to update online data on the church's website. Remember that many people begin their visit to your church by taking a look at your website for key information.

10. **Spruce up your building and grounds.** Promotion Sunday is the perfect day to put your best foot forward. Have carpets cleaned, make sure touch-up painting has been done, declutter classrooms, trim bushes, cut grass, and re-stripe the parking lot if needed.

FOCUS ATTENTION ON SUNDAY SCHOOL THROUGH YOUR WEBSITE

In the course of my work and ministry, I visit a lot of church websites each month. Dozens. Maybe more. Some are really great. Clean, efficient, and well planned, these websites provide easy-to-find information like Sunday and Wednesday schedules, core beliefs, and information about key ministries.

Sometimes, though, I've struggled to find the start time for a church's worship service. On other occasions I couldn't locate the Sunday School group options. That's frustrating. Focus attention on your church's Sunday School ministry by paying attention to the way you present your Sunday School ministry on the web. Remember that people are likely visiting your website long before they come to your church campus.

Don't forget that your Sunday School ministry is the ministry with the largest number of people connected to it. Lift it up! Bring it front and center. Tell people about it. Show them their options. Invite them to belong. As you focus people's attention on your church's Sunday School ministry, here are a few things that must be present on the Sunday School section of your church's website:

1. **Why groups?** Explain why the church even has Sunday School groups in the first place. Talk about the *why* before you talk about the *what*.

2. **What to expect.** Don't think that everyone knows what happens inside a group Bible study; they don't. You can relax anxious guests by telling them what happens in a typical group study. Promise them they will not be put on the spot, asked to pray out loud, or challenged to answer questions. Then make sure your group leaders abide by these basic ground rules when guests are present!

3. **A map of the facilities.** Some people like to get organized before they come onto your church campus, and getting a feel for the layout of your facilities is important to them.

4. **Location of each group.** Parents of children will especially appreciate knowing where their kids are in relation to the adult group they'll visit.

5. **The target audience of each group.** Every Bible study group should be assigned a certain people group to reach. That's easy in the student and kids ministries! It's more difficult when it comes to adult groups. Sometimes I see "The Joy Class" listed on a website, but I cannot tell who the group is supposed to reach! Is it for single adults or married? Young or old? Men or women? The more specific, the better.

6. **Security information (preschool and children).** Most churches now have a level of security in the areas of the church in which minor

children meet. If your church has a specific check-in/check-out system, tell guests what that looks like at your church. If they need to enter data into a computer prior to dropping off their children, tell them to budget a few extra minutes for that. No one likes surprises.

FOCUS ATTENTION ON SUNDAY SCHOOL FROM THE PULPIT

A good friend of mine, Dr. Tod Tanner, is pastor of Fair Haven Baptist Church in Shelbyville, Tennessee. He's my pastor now. He wants every member and guest to be in a group. I've heard him say something like this to the people:

- Thanks for being here today.
- I want to encourage you to get involved in a Bible study group.
- Our church is going to get bigger, so we must get smaller (in groups).
- Groups are really important to us here. Please connect with a Sunday School class.
- If your time is limited, go to Sunday School instead of hearing me preach.

Tod knows that people need guidance. They want to know the next step to take. Tod tells them, and he does so regularly. It's one of the ways Fair Haven Baptist Church focuses attention on the Sunday School. It's one of the reasons this church is growing.

Some pastors, like Pastor Tod, even go so far as to say something like, "I'm glad you're here in our worship service today. If you're going to give the church only one hour of your time on Sunday, I'd prefer you get connected to a group rather than hear me preach a sermon." This makes a big impression on members and guests. It tells them what's important to the pastor. If something is important to the pastor, it becomes important to the church. Whatever he sees as important almost always becomes important to the congregation.

If you want to breathe life into your church's Sunday School, focus attention on it from the pulpit. Encourage people to attend a group. Say this regularly. You may think you're saying it too much, but it takes time for people to grab hold of an idea. You constantly have new people in your services that need to hear this simple message. About the time you feel you've repeated the message too often is about the time your people will begin to understand and act on it.

5 MORE WAYS PASTORS CAN FOCUS ATTENTION ON SUNDAY SCHOOL

Pastors can and should be the church's number one champion and cheerleader for Sunday School. No one should be a bigger fan of Sunday School than the senior pastor. To focus even more attention on the Sunday School, pastors can do the following:

1. **Visit groups regularly.** These short visits won't take a lot of time, but they create a lot of emotional goodwill between the pastor and the people. If a pastor has the time, he should sit in on a full Bible study session. Then on occasion as the pastor preaches, he can say, "You know, just this morning when I was in John Q Public's adult group, I heard him say…" or "Today it brought joy to my heart to see all the children learning the Bible through our Sunday School ministry as I visited classes and talked to boys and girls." This will communicate volumes to members and guests.

2. **Attend fellowship events sponsored by Bible study groups.** Pastors are busy people, but occasionally spending an evening with a Bible study group when they have a party is a great way to get to know the members and guests.

3. **Preach a series of messages** on the importance of Bible study, relationships, and the Sunday School or small group ministry of your church. Don't assume that people in the congregation "get it." You'll want to help them understand the biblical basis for having a small-group Bible study strategy, how it benefits them, and why building relationships with others is so important to their spiritual growth and development.

4. **Speak at your church's annual group leader training event, lead a workshop, or just be present.** Pastors can help lift up Sunday School by clearing their calendars and setting aside this time. Participating in a training event with group leaders says that the Bible-teaching

ministry of your church is important, and so are its leaders. A pastor's absence communicates just the opposite, so "save the date."

5. **Schedule an annual commissioning service for group leaders.** Leading a group is hard work, and leading a group is not for everyone. Celebrate and support those men and women who tirelessly serve others by teaching God's Word. Schedule an annual commissioning service. Call attention to them and the importance of studying God's Word in groups.

If you want to breathe life into your Sunday School, focus attention on it.

FOR FURTHER THOUGHT

1. How have you focused attention on Sunday School this past year? Do you feel it was adequate? Why or why not?

2. Review your church's website. Is it clear that Sunday School is important? Can guests easily find the information they need before visiting for the first time?

3. If your church has a new members class, how effectively are you using it to focus attention on the importance of being involved in a Sunday School group?

4. Of the ways mentioned to focus attention on Sunday School, which are the most accessible? Where will you start?

04

ESSENTIAL 4: TRAIN THE LEADERS

I really like my hair stylist. I have a standing appointment with her every six weeks. Her name is Holly. She works at a guy's-only haircut salon. She takes notes and enters those into the computer each time I visit.

One day while Holly cut my hair, I noticed her license hanging on the wall inside her work station. I asked some questions about it. I discovered that for her to maintain her license, she has to go through regular training each year. No training, no job.

No kidding.

I remembered my father, who was a real estate broker. He owned and operated a small real estate company. Every summer he took classes to renew his broker's license. No training, no job.

No kidding.

And then there are my brother and sister-in-law, Mark and Brenda. Both are public school teachers, and both must participate in a minimum of 10 days of training per year to keep up their certification to teach. No training, no job.

No kidding.

Police. Firefighters. Lawyers. Teachers. Realtors. Electricians. Hair stylists. The guy who makes my tuna sandwich. What do they have in common? Their jobs require ongoing training. If you think about it, there is almost no job on the planet that does not require an employee to have regular, ongoing training.

Why is it that we recruit teachers to lead Bible study groups but do not provide regular times of training? In church after church, training has been decreased or eliminated. And we wonder why Sunday School needs a breath of life breathed into it? If other industries require their people to be trained in order to continue in their profession, why is it that the church, which handles the life-changing Word of God, does not provide more ongoing training for its leaders who handle the gospel week after week? One state convention discovered that 98% of the top fifty fastest growing churches in their state provided training for their Sunday School leaders. Steve Parr, a Sunday School leader in Georgia, asks, "Could it be that the reason they are the fastest growing Sunday Schools is because they have trained and skilled leaders? That certainly is at least a portion of the explanation. These churches were of all sizes and in all types of community settings. The fact that they train their leaders was one of the most common practices related to Sunday School."[20]

If you want to breathe life into your Sunday School, you must train the leaders. Ed Stetzer wrote about "comeback churches" in his book by the same title. He and co-author Mike Dodson identified factors that caused churches that formerly plateaued to grow again. "While everything rises and falls on leadership, it would be more accurate to say that everything rises and falls on leadership that develops other leaders...This process must be built into a systematic, intentional strategy to develop more groups and train new leaders. This provides a foundation for sustainable growth."[21]

AN OBLIGATION TO TRAIN?

I recently read a book on leadership in the church by Aubrey Malphurs and Will Mancini. They made an important observation about training. They stated that if we are going to call people into a leadership role, we are obligated to provide training. Obligated. They explain, "If we ask our people to lead any ministry of the church, we're responsible to provide them with continual leadership training. If we can't do this, we have no business asking them to serve, doing both them and the ministry an injustice. Without ongoing training, our recruits will struggle and often fail, and the rest of the ministry will experience the effects in the resulting leadership vacuum."[22]

Pastors equip. That's Ephesians 4:11-12. Training is a form of equipping. For the many years I served on church staff in a full-time pastoral role, I provided ongoing training for group leaders. I could not, in good conscience, ask someone to serve without providing training and encouragement.

A MOST IMPORTANT DISCOVERY

The Georgia Baptist Convention surveyed over 2,500 churches in that state, asking the question, "How frequently do you train your group leaders?" The growth of those churches over a four-year period was examined and the results were tabulated.

An important discovery was made. Churches that provided ongoing training either quarterly or monthly grew at a rate in excess of 13% during that time period. That should be enough to make anyone in church leadership pay close attention.

Other factors may have contributed to the growth of these Sunday Schools, but the one factor we can identify with certainty is the frequency at which training was conducted.

Churches with less frequent training (annually) grew at a much smaller rate (4.2%), and those churches that chose not to train at all actually declined by 2.1%.[23]

Training matters. If you want to breathe life into your Sunday School, you must train the leaders.

FREQUENCY OF LEADERSHIP TRAINING	NUMBER OF CHURCHES	CHURCHES IN CATEGORY (%)	AVERAGE SUNDAY SCHOOL ATTENDANCE		
			1999	2002	DIFFERENCE
WEEKLY	88	3.5	20,430	21,725	+6.3
MONTHLY	202	7.9	59,999	68,045	+13.4
QUARTERLY	314	12.3	46,569	53,004	+13.8
ANNUALLY	540	21.2	64,482	67,167	+4.2
OTHER	367	14.4	37,107	37,412	+0.8
NEVER	1033	40.6	47,733	46,727	-2.1
TOTAL*	2544	100			

SOURCE: Table has been abbreviated from Research Services, Georgia Baptist Convention, February 2002

*There were 2544 of 3008 churches that respond to the leadership question: "How often do you conduct Sunday School leadership training?"

THE REAL PROBLEM IS...

If I said the name Arthur Flake, would you know who he is or what he is famous for? Because he lived and served in the early part of the twentieth century, you may not be familiar with his life and work. He was a lay Sunday School director at his church in Winona, Mississippi. He developed a five-step formula for growing the Sunday School. His church experienced such success that he was asked to lead the Sunday School Board's Sunday School division. Here is what Arthur Flake had to say about "the real problem" in Sunday School way back in 1922; it still applies to us today: "The preceding discussion brings us to the real need, which is an organization of sufficient size made up of intelligent, skillful, Spirit-filled men and women who will bring the pupils into the Sunday School, teach them the Word of God, and win them to Christ. Thus, the real problem of building a great Sunday School anywhere, under all conditions and circumstances, is one of developing trained officers and teachers...They largely determine the quality of the teaching done. They set the gauge for the soul-winning spirit and fervor of the Sunday School. The quality of work done by the teachers will not, cannot, rise higher than the ability displayed by the officers in the administration of the affairs of the Sunday School. It is impossible to build an efficient Sunday School with an ignorant, indifferent, untrained, lazy, cold set of officers. No corps of teachers can overcome a handicap like that."[24]

I like the way Mr. Flake puts an emphasis on training the most significant and largest group of leaders in the church—Bible study leaders! He realized that without a trained corp of leaders, the Sunday School would not be healthy. As he mentioned, training starts at the top. Those who lead Sunday School must believe in the importance of training.

Recently, I led a time of training and encouragement for the group leaders at my church in the Nashville area. Fair Haven Baptist Church now has a one-year history of implementing ongoing teacher training. The results? A year ago, the Sunday School averaged 198 people. Today, it has had a high day of 298. My prediction? The church will soon be breaking the 300 barrier regularly. Training may not be responsible for all of the growth, but it is responsible for part of it.

IF YOU BUILD IT

Some individuals have lost hope that teachers will attend training today. Not me. I am a firm believer in ongoing training. Will busy people today come to training that is sponsored by your church? The answer is yes if two things happen:

- **The training is done with quality.** This doesn't mean it has to be expensive. It just has to be done decently and in order. Start on time. End on time. Have a clear agenda for the meeting. Don't waste people's time at your training events! If you can communicate something via email, do it. Save the training time for things that are of critical importance—things that can only be communicated face-to-face.

- **Group leaders are recruited with the expectation they will participate in ongoing training.** "A key to regular attendance at the meeting is that you recruit leaders with the understanding that attendance is expected. You will find that many persons actually respond positively to the greater level of demand. Most churches would not consider having a choir that did not meet for rehearsal... In similar fashion, it is difficult to think that we would entrust the teaching of God's Word to persons who did not have the commitment to meet..."[25]

OPTIONS FOR TRAINING GROUP LEADERS

You simply cannot afford not to train your group leaders. I've worked with churches that had no history of ongoing training. The pastor of one church in particular asked me to craft an annual training plan for the upcoming year. I developed a plan to train group leaders four times throughout the year; it was something they could afford to do and could rally their group leaders to do as well.

It just takes a little thought, a little money, a place on the church calendar, and support by the pastor and staff. Crafting a training plan for the year is something every church can do. How might your church go about the important task of training its group leaders if you haven't been in the habit of providing it?

Here are ten training options for churches of all sizes and shapes. There's no reason any church should be without a plan for training.

1. **Weekly training.** Fewer and fewer churches do this today. Those that do typically offer only one curriculum in all of their adult groups (or student and kids groups). The focus is on helping group leaders prepare to teach the upcoming lesson. Lesson preparation is normally the reason for these kinds of meetings.

2. **Monthly training.** This typically involves age-group training. Adult, student, and leaders of kids groups meet in separate training sessions. Each group participates in training designed for the age groups they lead.

3. **Quarterly training.** Churches that practice this kind of training bring all group leaders together in one room to hear a message designed for them all. A guest speaker is frequently brought in to motivate the volunteer workers. Sometimes a video series is used for the training. On other occasions the pastor or Sunday School director delivers the training to the leaders.

4. **Training opportunities offered at the local level.** Local associations of churches often schedule training events in the fall, spring, and summer months. Check with your local association to discover what their training options are. These tend to be affordable, low-cost events.

5. **Training opportunities offered at the state level.** Like local associations, state conventions offer training events as well. These take place year-round, so check with your state convention about the training opportunities being provided this year. These tend to be affordable, but often require traveling to a regional location.

6. **Regional training opportunities.** The company I work for provides regional training events, and we utilize professional trainers and church practitioners to deliver high-quality workshops aimed at improving teaching in all kinds of groups.

7. **Personal training.** There is nothing to keep group leaders from creating their own annual plan for personal training. This may include a workshop, the reading of books related to a particular area of ministry, or something else.

8. Training in triads or quads. Some church leaders place group leaders in smaller three-person triads or four-person quads. The group is asked to read a book or article provided by the church staff leader to whom they report. The group then gets together once or twice to discuss what they've learned at a time convenient to them.

9. Training done in a retreat setting. A retreat setting allows everyone to focus on the training and relationship-building that takes place when you get away for a few days.

10. Training done by partnering with another church. Churches are learning they can partner with one another and share the costs of bringing in a guest presenter. This makes training affordable for both churches (or perhaps three or four churches).

POTENTIAL LEADER TRAINING

Your church has two groups of leaders: current leaders and future ones. It's important to provide ongoing training for current group leaders. But it's equally important to have a plan to onboard new group leaders. Some people call this a "pipeline" of leadership.

However you choose to think about it, the future of your Sunday School is at stake. You cannot start new groups without new leaders. You cannot replace current group leaders without new ones, either. "Invariably churches that consistently do effective Sunday School work train and equip their Sunday School leaders. No better place to begin can be found than with persons who have not yet determined where they would like to work in Sunday School. No better training can be offered than to help persons select an area in which they would most enjoy serving in Sunday School and then to equip them for service.

Recall a trip during which you stayed in an unfamiliar house. Do you remember feeling insecure as you walked across a dark room in the middle of the night? You did not know what was ahead of you or what you might run into. Many new Sunday School workers feel that way. They suddenly find themselves tossed into a new place of service. Like waking up in the middle of the night, they do not know what to expect or where they are going. Prior to beginning their service, potential Sunday School workers need to be enlightened on what to expect in each area of Sunday School work. Instead of walking in fear, potential workers can walk in confidence because they know what is expected of them."[26]

7 TIMES TO SCHEDULE TRAINING

You have several options that might make sense depending upon the culture of your church. Here are some of the more popular options:

1. **Friday night.** Normally this is used only for special occasion training where a guest speaker is hired to come to the church and encourage and train your leaders. A meal is often provided by the church, catered perhaps by a local restaurant.

2. **Saturday morning.** Popular in the past, churches have struggled to get leaders to attend Saturday morning training because of the influence of kids sports and the need for mom and dad to do house and yard work, plus other weekend chores and activities.

3. **Sunday, after morning worship.** This one is growing in popularity. People are already on campus, so why not ask them to stay through the lunch hour and slightly beyond? Churches have found success when they provide a noon meal for the leaders and their families, followed by 90-120 minutes of training. It doesn't require another night out of the house, and people don't have to sacrifice a Saturday.

4. **Sunday afternoon, before evening activities.** Many churches still find that a late afternoon time of training works for their people.

5. **Wednesday evenings.** This may be a good time for mid-week training, but you may run into leaders who cannot attend because of work schedules, traffic, kids sports, and general fatigue.

6. **Sunday mornings.** This is the one that I transitioned to when I was on church staff leading the education and discipleship ministries. You might be asking yourself, "How does this work?" Actually, pretty well! I "time shifted" our training to Sunday mornings when many of my group leaders could no longer attend mid-week training. Once a month I met with the leaders of all my adult Bible study groups. We ate breakfast together, and then moved into a time of training during the Sunday School hour. I can hear your question! "If your

teachers were with you for training, who was leading the Bible studies that day?" All of my group leaders recruited apprentice teachers and turned over the teaching responsibility to them once a month. It had the side benefit of preparing a new generation of group leaders for service. No childcare was required because the kids of my teachers were in Sunday School. No additional nights out of the house were needed. It worked for us at that time and place. Perhaps it might work in your context too.

7. **Any time.** Churches are learning to use YouTube,® Vimeo,® Zoom,® and other digital delivery services so that group leaders get training at a time that is convenient for them.

A DIFFERENT WAY OF THINKING

If you are becoming convinced that training your group leaders is a good thing, you'll want to make sure you budget enough funds to make training possible. Refer back to the chapter on feeding the Sunday School financially.

Don't think of training as an expense. Think of it as an essential investment in your church's future. The finance team, deacons, and members must place a high value on training, which includes the funds to make it happen with quality. If something is viewed as an investment, you protect and nurture it, recognizing its value. If it's an expense, you cut it when times get tough.

Sunday School is most likely your church's largest ministry. It involves more people than any other ministry in the church. It touches every person—both member and guest, young and old. It deserves the funds to train its leaders.

To properly budget for training, make certain you've thought through these annual expenses related to training:

- Guest speakers
- Travel and lodging for guest speakers
- Honorariums for guest speakers
- Food (meals and snacks) for the group leaders
- Printing/copying supplies

- Name tags, markers, pens, etc.
- Decorations
- Videos, books, and other resources needed to conduct the training

DEVELOPING A TRAINING BUDGET

Let's say that my church wanted to start training its group leaders. It became aware of the Georgia training research and decided to train leaders once a quarter. To create the budget for training, the leadership team decided to do the following to train its seventy-five group leaders.

1. Schedule four quarterly training events on Sunday afternoons.
2. Purchase a video training series for $139 and use three of the twelve training videos in the first year.
3. Hire a team of trainers to come to the church and provide training by age groups in August and engage group leaders in a live training event.

The budget for these four trainings would be:

- $139 (video series)
- $3,000 (live training/honorariums/travel/guest presenters)
- $600 (food and snacks for three quarterly video-driven training events)
- $1,250 (catered meal from a local restaurant) for the live training event

Adding up these items leads me to a total of $4,989 for the year. Dividing that by four events equals an average of $1,247.25 per event. Dividing it again by seventy-five group leaders equals $16.63 per person, per event. Dividing that again by three (three months per quarter) requires that the church invest $5.54 per month per leader into the training of each of its group leaders. Doing the math one more time and dividing the $5.54 by thirty days in a month reveals that the church can train its group leaders by investing just $.18 per day for each group leader.

That doesn't sound so bad after all, does it? In fact, it now sounds completely within reach.

By the way, the plan I've detailed above is the plan that I am working on for my church, the one where Pastor Tod is our senior pastor. Until recently, the church had no training budget, but we believed in the value of starting ongoing, quarterly training. We'll ultimately grow into a more elaborate training plan. We'll learn to crawl, then walk, then run.

TRAINING ON A SMALL BUDGET

Suppose you read the last example and agreed that training your church's leaders is necessary. But even so, your church is not in a financial position to adopt this kind of training budget. What should you do? Decide that training is just too expensive? Give up on the dream of starting ongoing training? Absolutely not! If you are tight on funds, here are some ways to provide quality training on a shoestring budget.

1. Provide training that does not require food. Start at 9 a.m. on a Saturday and end at 11:30 a.m. You won't need to provide breakfast or lunch, maybe just coffee, water, and soda.

2. Call on experts in your congregation to lead training. There's a great chance you have people in your congregation who are teachers by trade, business leaders, or trainers in their companies. Give them a topic and plenty of lead time, and invite them to help you train the church's group leaders. Instead of paying them an honorarium, purchase a gift card to their favorite restaurant. That's a lot less expensive, and they'll appreciate the gesture.

3. Use free resources. Did you know that LifeWay's former Sunday School Director, David Francis, wrote a dozen annual training books on Sunday School? They are all available for free, along with free conference plans and PowerPoint® slide shows! You might want to check them out at lifeway.com/davidfrancis. You'd have over a decade of free training materials if you used them.

FINAL THOUGHTS

With all of this in mind, I'll wrap up this chapter by reminding you of the main reasons to budget, schedule, and execute ongoing training for group leaders.

1. **Group leaders often determine whether or not people get assimilated into Bible study groups.** Your assimilation process depends, in part, on guests having a good experience in the classroom.

If your teachers are well-trained, they'll do a better job teaching and guiding people in Bible study. Guests will be more likely to connect with your church.

2. **Turnover will be reduced.** As the confidence and competence of group leaders rise, they will be less inclined to quit teaching. Competence breeds confidence. If you are a pastor or church staff leader, you'll save valuable recruiting time and be able to focus on other important aspects of ministry. When I led my church's education ministries, Sunday School turnover in the adult groups was often zero.

3. **Training and growth have a strong correlation.** Look at Georgia's chart again. How would you like to experience consistent growth? If your church committed to ongoing training and you began to grow again, what could you do with the additional people and the higher level of tithes and offerings that will also come?

4. **Excellence won't happen without it.** Too many churches settle for mediocrity in their groups ministries. George Barna, in his book *The Frog in The Kettle*, said, "Churches must take a hard look at everything they do. In today's marketplace, people are critical and unforgiving and often give a church only one chance to impress. In this kind of environment, churches would be better off focusing on a few things with excellence rather than many things with mediocrity."[27] You may be thinking, "Wait a minute. We just do not have enough people at our church who can serve as group leaders." Although that's a fairly common evaluation of a church's potential, let me share the words of a Sunday School hero who saw things a little differently. About the lack of workers, he said, "This is an imaginary difficulty, for every church has within its membership enough teachers and officers to take care of the Sunday School...To be sure they are not trained and efficient, but they have been saved and they are good raw material out of which fine officers and teachers can be made. They need to be trained and put to work in the Sunday School."[28]

FOR FURTHER THOUGHT

1. What is your reaction to the statement that you are obligated to train people if you ask them to participate in a ministry? Do you agree or disagree? Why?

2. What is the biggest hurdle to overcome if you were to establish a training schedule for your group leaders next year?

3. How will you deal with resistance to training on the part of volunteers? What would your plan be for dealing with leaders whose first reaction is to say "no" to the training you want to provide?

4. Stop and do: In fifteen minutes, write out a training plan for your church's group leaders similar to the one mentioned in this chapter. Later, refine it, share it, budget for it, and implement it.

ESSENTIAL 5: START NEW GROUPS

I love the community where I live. It's grown exponentially over the last ten years. New people have moved into my neighborhood. New businesses are constantly moving into my town. Over the past month I've frequented some of those retailers. Many of them weren't here a year ago.

These businesses, even though they are vastly different, have one thing in common: they started small, and they expanded. They grew. And there was a method to their madness. When McDonald's® expanded its first restaurant, it didn't tear the place down and build a bigger one on the same spot. That might have worked to reach a few more customers, but they found a better strategy: franchising. Franchising brought exponential growth to the company. Tearing down that first restaurant would have only added growth. Franchising allowed them to multiply their growth. I first heard this concept of franchising applied to Sunday School at the Ridgecrest Conference Center in North Carolina. Friend and colleague Allan Taylor addressed a gathering of Sunday School leaders and challenged churches to franchise their groups. We've learned over the years that most groups don't like hearing the terms "split, divide, or birth." The latest term, franchising, is a much friendlier term that everyone understands.

Growth has taken place in countless businesses because they built new buildings, trained new teams, and opened their doors to customers they'd never reached before through the strategy of franchising. Effective churches have discovered the benefits of franchising groups. They have learned the value of starting new groups, and it's become part of their DNA. Many churches haven't started a new group in years. They don't franchise groups. Those Sunday Schools are in decline. Those are the ones that need life breathed into them. According to David Francis, "Ideas abound about how a Sunday School, a church, or the larger Kingdom of God grows. All of those theories can be reduced to this most basic principle: Start new units. New preaching/teaching points. New missions. New churches. New ministry teams. New small groups. New discipleship groups. New Sunday School classes."[29]

Churches that haven't started new groups have adopted a "let's tear it down and build a bigger one" mindset. Rather than starting new groups, groups are combined when a teacher steps out of leadership, or guests are sent to large groups that just keep getting larger. That's growth by addition. What the church needs today is growth by multiplication. The lack of "franchising" Bible study groups has cost the church much needed growth today.

Ed Stetzer and Mike Dodson, the authors of *Comeback Churches,* emphasized the importance of starting new groups in their book. They cited research that centered on more than 300 churches that were once stagnant and in decline. Those churches found new life and vitality in part by starting new groups. "Comeback churches made it a priority to start new groups. The ones that utilized Sunday School started new classes and carved out more space for them to meet. In some cases, they built. But in every case, comeback leaders found a way to connect more people in biblical community."[30]

GOD-SIZED GROWTH

In November 1992 I quit a part-time job to become a mission church's education pastor. The church opened its doors around Thanksgiving, and I began my last semester of seminary in January. I told my wife to kiss her mother goodbye. I was confident that when I graduated in May, a bigger church would scoop me up. I wasn't planning on staying at this little mission church that had forty-four people in Sunday School on opening day. But I sure am thankful the Lord chose to leave me there for ten years!

This little mission church didn't stay little for very long. We found ourselves in the path of growth, and from my seminary and Sunday School training background, I knew the right thing to do was to start new groups.

So we did. We started new groups. We franchised classes. The Sunday School grew. The church became known for having the fastest growing Sunday School in Texas for a number of years. We received awards. The Southern Baptist Convention and the North American Mission Board honored the church as the Outstanding New Church Start in 1994. We were blessed. God was at work.

Starting new groups is what helped make the growth possible. We had groups into which we funneled all the new people we reached. God added to our number weekly. When I left this church to go to the second church I served, I left behind a Sunday School that had grown to over 2,400 members. The church had purchased seven portable buildings in which we placed many Sunday School groups. We built a multi-million-dollar education building. We started a second Sunday School hour. Then we started a third hour of Sunday School.

When these things didn't hold us, I rented a school one mile from the church, and we placed adult groups there. When that didn't hold us, I asked members to allow us to start groups in their homes, and several opened their homes to us on Sunday mornings. It was not unusual to see an entire group gather at the church campus for worship, then walk together one or two blocks to have a time of Bible study in someone's living room.

If you want to breathe life into your Sunday School, you must start new groups. You must franchise. Starting new groups and franchising existing ones does good things for your church.

1. **New groups reach underserved people.** Every church's Bible teaching ministry (call it Sunday School, LIFE groups, or whatever other term you like) has gaps. There are some people who simply don't have a great place to attend a Bible study. Look around your congregation and community to see what kinds of people wouldn't have a place if they came to your church to study the Bible in a group. New groups provide a place for the underserved.

2. **New groups enlarge the church.** It's a fact that new groups will reach, on average, ten new people. If you wanted to grow your church's Sunday School by thirty people this year, you'd need to start three new groups, plus maybe one or two more to cover the "churn"

that takes place each year. (Churn is the number of people who move off, leave the church, die, etc.)

3. **New groups encourage people to use their spiritual gifts.** New groups provide fresh soil in which leaders can be planted. Given a place to grow their leadership skills and use their spiritual gifts, they blossom. An apprentice teacher who teaches an adult group once or twice every six months will not fully develop as a teacher-leader until he or she has a group to lead. New groups also give group members a place to serve and use their spiritual gifts.

4. **New groups create a "LEGO®" factor.** New groups filled with new people give people a place to relationally connect. When you send a guest to an older, established group, you send that person into an environment in which people are already "LEGO'd up." They have connected with one another as friends. They've done ministry together. They're tight. A guest has little or no chance of connecting to people in that group. The opposite is true in a new group. People are still open relationally. Like a LEGO block, they have open connection points and can link up with one another relationally.

5. **New groups have positive financial implications for the church.** Every church has a per capita giving number that is consistent. New groups, properly started, will add ten new people on average to the Sunday School ministry. If a church's per capita giving is $35, I can be confident that one new group of ten people will give about $350 per week on average. Multiplied by fifty-two weeks in a year, the annual impact of starting one new group is $18,200. It's a side-benefit of multiplying Great Commission work the church should be doing already.

THE COST OF STARTING NEW GROUPS

If you'll recall, in an earlier chapter I wrote about the need to budget for Sunday School. From time to time, I hear a concern raised by a staff member that goes like this: "We just can't afford to start new groups. Curriculum is expensive. We'd have to buy some new tables and chairs. I just don't see how we can afford to do this."

To that person I'd say, "I don't see how you can afford not to start new groups!"

Let's continue to use the example above. Let's assume that your church has a $35 per capita giving. (In reality, it is probably higher.)

You decide to start a new group. That means you need to provide that group with something to study each week. The company I work for produces ongoing Bible studies for Sunday School groups and can resource each member of the group (ten people in our example) with a Personal Study Guide. The group leader would also have a Leader Guide that gives him or her step-by-step instructions on how to lead the weekly study. The group leader can also receive a Leader Pack, something that contains posters, charts, maps, and other tools for leading and guiding the group's Bible study. All of this can be purchased for approximately $65 per quarter per group. That's just $260 per year to equip one group.

Remember that a new group of ten will add about $18,000 of tithes and offerings (assuming a $35 per capita). Now subtract the cost of curriculum, and subtract the cost of chairs, a couple of tables, and a coffee pot. You're still in the black! Probably $15,000 in the black. And you are accomplishing Kingdom purposes as you reach new people. You cannot afford *not* to start new groups.

WHEN TO START NEW GROUPS

In the book *Great Expectations*, the author reminds us of the expectation every group should have placed on it—the expectation of starting another group. "A great expectations Sunday School class always expects to plant new classes."[31] Great groups start new groups. If you were going to start new groups, when would you do it? I have observed there are at least four optimal times per year.

1. **At the start of the new year.** Many people come back to church after the busy Christmas holidays. They are ready to get back into the swing of things. Other people make resolutions as they start the new year, and among those are getting regular in a Bible study group. New groups started at the beginning of the new year can reach people who are trying to reconnect with the church.

2. **A Sunday or two after Easter.** Just as people come back to the church at the first of the year, others come back to the church for Easter services. Promote the new groups several weeks leading up to Easter, and have a list of groups and a registration form in the Easter worship bulletin. Make it easy for people to express interest in getting signed up for one of your new groups. Simply have the guests place the registration forms in the offering plate on Easter, and give their contact information to the new group leaders that afternoon so that follow-up can begin on Monday.

3. **Back-to-school time in August.** There's no doubt your church experiences the "summer slumps." Members take vacations, and July is typically the month with the lowest average attendance. But just wait until August; the people return in large numbers, excited about the start of school, football, and other activities. New groups often get off to a great start at this time of the year as people slide back into routines.

4. **Any month when attendance spikes.** Keep track of your Sunday School attendance over time, and you'll see attendance patterns develop. You can quickly identify the one or two months of the year when attendance spikes at your church, and that's the time to start new groups. I tracked the attendance patterns of the first church I served, and we always spiked in August, September, and January. The second church I served had a slightly different pattern; it spiked in February (probably coinciding with the pastor's sermon series that occurred after the first of the year). Get to know your church's attendance pattern, and you'll know exactly what month (or months) are best for starting new groups.

Allan Taylor loves it when the Sunday School starts new groups. He has these words of wisdom about the timing. "Starting new classes should be done at times that are conducive for them to experience success. Most new classes cannot overcome immediate failure. Therefore, it is best to start new classes at peak attendance times of the year."[32]

NEW GROUPS, NEW LEADERS, AND BAD ENLISTMENT

New groups must have new leaders. If you are going to start new groups, you are going to have to enlist new group leaders. There's just no way around it. And you need to enlist the right way, not the wrong way.

I am able to grin and laugh as I recall and tell this true story of how my wife and I were first recruited to teach an eighth grade girls Sunday School class. It wasn't funny at the time.

My wife and I had been married only a few months. We made a commitment to begin our marriage by finding, attending, and becoming involved in a church. We found the right church and began attending Sunday morning and night, plus Wednesday nights. We were there whenever the doors were open.

One of the church's staff, the student pastor, approached my wife and I as we made our way through the crowded church foyer one Sunday morning.

"Hey," he said, "You two are here every week. You'd make great teachers. How would you like to teach a group in the student Sunday School?"

I looked at my wife, and she looked back at me. I looked at the student pastor. "I guess we could do that," I said. "Great," he replied! "Here are your teaching materials! You start next week. Meet us at Fellowship Hall at 9 a.m." And then he disappeared into the crowd. I never even got to look at the Leader Guide he held at his side.

We stood there dumbfounded. I wondered to myself, "What just happened?" And so we began our teaching ministry. The next Sunday we showed up ready to teach. Or at least I thought we were ready.

We were given a group of young ladies to teach. I was horrible. I cannot believe they didn't all bail on us. We got better in time. The girls hung in there with us.

And that's exactly how I was recruited to teach. Not exactly the textbook way to be recruited, but it had a happy ending thanks to the Lord. And to this student pastor's credit, he held weekly teacher's meetings that helped me improve quickly.

NEW GROUPS, NEW LEADERS, AND ENLISTMENT DONE RIGHT

If you are going to start new groups, you must enlist group leaders. If you're going to enlist people, you should do it the right way. Most of us don't enjoy the enlistment process. It's slow. It can be uncomfortable to hear "no" from the people we're recruiting to a leadership role. We avoid it. We procrastinate.

There are things you can do to make the enlistment process better for everyone. Would you like to increase the number of people who say "yes" to opportunities to serve? If that's your desire, then here are some ways to properly recruit someone.

1. **Start with prayer.** When Jesus and His disciples came upon a field that was ready to be harvested, He used this powerful visual aid to tell His disciples that the solution to the enormous task of reaching people with the gospel began not by adding extra shifts, working longer days, or recruiting more people to help. He told His disciples the solution was to pray. They were to pray for their Heavenly Father to send out workers into the fields. The particular word for "pray" in this verse is a word that means "to beg because of a lack or need." It describes a prayer born of desperation. It is the prayer of a person who has realized his limited capacity and has turned to his Heavenly Father for help. Is this the way you pray for workers? Proper recruitment begins with proper prayer.

2. **Set an appointment.** We set an appointment when we need to see the doctor. We set an appointment for a haircut. We set an appointment for an oil change. When it comes to recruiting new group leaders, always set an appointment. An appointment says, "This is important. I value your time."

3. **Avoid "all-call" announcements.** If you throw a net into the ocean and drag it for a while, what will you find when you pull it onto the deck of the boat? You'll find that you caught all kinds of fish. Some you might keep. Others you'll throw back. In church, making an all-call announcement from the pulpit is like dragging a net. You'll catch a few good fish, but you will also catch some that you will want

to throw back. When a person hears an all-call announcement and volunteers, they might not be the right person to fill the position. If they're not, then you risk doing damage when you turn them down.

4. **Ask for a specific time commitment.** Don't let the person you are recruiting think that the role is open-ended. Tell them how long you are expecting them to serve. I always recruited group leaders for one year at a time. I realize that people sometimes want to volunteer for shorter periods of time, but when it comes to group leadership, I believe a one-year commitment is best.

5. **Clarify the win.** We've covering that in the next chapter!

6. **Provide sample resources.** Why would you want to allow a potential group leader to review the resources he or she is being asked to teach? Because that person needs to know they don't have to create their own studies from scratch each week.

7. **Provide a list of training opportunities.** If you are on the receiving end of a visit about becoming a group leader, how comforting it is to hear that your staff leader who's recruiting you has a plan for training you throughout the year! When I served on staff, I provided group leaders with a list of all scheduled training events as we gathered for our big annual training event in August. That training kicked off the new Sunday School year, and my group leaders received a list of potential training events they could attend, all the way through August of the next year. They were able to plan which events they would attend up to a year in advance.

8. **Agree to work together to start a new group.** If you've ever met any resistance on the part of a group leader to "splitting his class" to start another one, you know recruiting a person with that expectation in mind is the way to change your organization. As current group leaders step down and change ministry roles, recruit the new group leader with the expectation that you will work together as a team to "franchise" the group and start another one. Get buy-in at the front end, and you'll be more effective in starting new groups.

9. **Use a leader covenant.** A leader covenant doesn't have to be long. If you have more than six or seven items, it's probably too long. Leader

covenants "clarify the win" and tell group leaders what they should be doing to succeed. It's a document that can be reviewed occasionally with individual group leaders to see if there's been any mission drift.

BUSTING MYTHS

A myth is "an unfounded or false notion."[33] I wonder how many myths we've believed with regard to Sunday School, especially when it comes to Bible study groups? What things might we believe are true but are really not? What if these Sunday School myths keep us from having a vibrant, healthy, growing Sunday School? Let's challenge some of the more common myths about starting groups.

> **Myth #1: Large groups should be left alone.** Sometimes a new group grows exponentially. Large groups can be intimidating. It's not easy to approach the teacher-leader of a large group and try to convince him to "split his group." Many a well-meaning pastor or staff leader has run into the buzz saw of a group leader who had the mentality that "bigger is better" and opposed any attempt to dilute his group by sending people out of it to start new ones. Look for group leaders who have a "catch and release" mindset. You need group leaders who will catch people but release them to serve and start new groups, not stand in opposition to starting a new group.

> **Myth #2: Smaller groups aren't healthy groups.** I have always cautioned group leaders and group members about thinking that "bigger is better." Sometimes a group starts small and remains small over time. Releasing people to start new groups is one of the signs of a healthy group. If you are a group leader, think of your group as a "clearing house" and not a storehouse of people. A small (or smaller) group may be one of the healthiest groups in the church because it continually starts "daughter" groups that reach new people.

> **Myth #3: "Splitting a group" ruins fellowship.** I've seen groups start new groups many times. Rarely, if ever, did starting a new group "ruin" the fellowship of a group. In fact, just the opposite took place. It became easier for the people who remained in the parent group to form new relationships, and it was certainly easier for guests to build

relationships with the members there. The same was true in the new group that was started. The pioneers who started the group banded together and grew close as they did God's will to reach new people. As they reached potential new group members, the newer people were drawn into relationships and were assimilated much more quickly than they would have been in a larger group.

Myth #4: If a group doesn't start a new one, another one will. Not always. Sunday School groups must adopt a "missionary mindset." The longer a group has been together, the more inwardly focused it tends to become. New groups tend to grow faster and reach more people than older, established groups, so it's very important that all groups make starting new ones a priority. You can't assume the group next door is committed to doing that. The group of which I am currently a member was birthed from a large class where the average attendance was approximately forty people. That class took responsibility for starting a new group, sent out a handful of adults, and now sixteen to eighteen of us gather each week for Bible study, prayer, and ministry, just a few steps away from our parent class.

If you want to breathe life into Sunday School, you must start new groups. The most successful companies in the country have learned this lesson. Learn from their example and franchise your groups.

FOR FURTHER THOUGHT

1. What underserved or unreached people need a group just for them in your Sunday School? What possibilities do you see for growth?

2. Based on your church's attendance pattern, when would be an optimal time (or times) to start new groups?

3. If your church started several new groups and you suddenly had a new infusion of tithes and offerings, where might you invest those extra dollars for ministry? Dream a little!

4. For whom should you be praying that the Lord would open their heart and mind to the possibility of starting a new group (or groups)? Stop and pray for that person or persons right now.

06

ESSENTIAL 6: CLARIFY THE WIN

Perhaps one of the most overlooked needs in Sunday School today is the need for volunteer leaders to know what a "win" is. A win is something essential to the success of the Sunday School.

The authors of *7 Practices of Effective Ministry* explain, "Countless leaders have innocently sabotaged their church by leading people in the wrong direction. And the fault lies with an organization that has not been systematic about defining and clarifying what a win really is."[34]

If you asked group leaders to define the purpose of Sunday School, you'd hear these kinds of responses. It's what I've heard when I've asked the question. These are ways that people try to articulate what winning is to them in Sunday School.

- "Sunday School is about teaching the Bible. It's about learning God's Word."
- "Sunday School should be about knowing people. We need to know each other's hurts, stories, and needs. We should be a house of prayer."
- "Sunday School is about having fun. You know, having parties and fellowships and enjoying each other."
- "Sunday School is about _____." (You fill in the blank, because it's probably already been said before.)

And therein lies the challenge in so many churches and in so many Sunday School groups. How does anyone know if they are winning at Sunday School?

IN THE ABSENCE OF A CLEARLY DEFINED "WIN"

Scripture demonstrates that in the absence of leadership, people will do whatever they deem to be right (Judg. 21:25). In the absence of a clearly defined win, the leaders in the Sunday School might take off in numerous directions, some good and some not so good.

I first learned about the concept of the "win" from *7 Practices of Effective Ministry*. The authors spelled out what happens if pastors and other church leaders do not clarify the win for their people:

"The church should be more determined than any other organization to 'clarify the win' simply because the stakes are so much higher. Eternity hangs in the balance...Clarifying the win simply means communicating to your team what is really important, what really matters...The best way to leverage the collective power of your team is to make sure that everyone knows what it means to 'score.' Nothing hinders morale more than when team members with separate agendas are pulling against one another...If the win is unclear, you may force those in leadership roles to define winning in their own terms...If you don't define winning for your ministry leaders, they will define it for themselves.

It doesn't take very long for leaders to take over a class, start a new program, begin an innovative ministry, and rally a crowd to follow them. They may only be a degree or two off track, but given enough time they will miss the target by miles. It's not that they're intentionally being defiant or difficult, they're just being leaders...Misalignment usually happens gradually. And if it goes unchecked, it can wreak havoc on an organization. Like the wheels on a car pulling against each other, misalignment will ultimately ruin the tires and waste enormous amounts of fuel."[35]

If your church isn't clearly communicating the purpose and goals of the Sunday School, it won't get the results you desire. To breathe life into Sunday School, clarify what it means for your team to win.

CLARITY IS CRITICAL

The group leaders in your Sunday School are waiting for you to tell them how to win. Your Sunday School can become healthier and more effective than ever before if you simply clarify your expectations of groups.

Clarifying the win can breathe new life into your Sunday School. Here's how it will help.

1. **"Clarifying the win" helps group leaders say no.** Just as important as saying yes to some activities is knowing when to say no to good opportunities that are outside the goals set for your groups. A group leader should know instantly if he should say yes to an opportunity because it aligns with the "win" his church leaders have established.

2. **"Clarifying the win" helps you set a budget.** If your church has determined that a "win" is for people to be discipled, then it follows that somewhere in the church's budget, dollars must be set aside for Bible study materials. If a "win" is for groups to regularly fellowship together, then someone on church staff must budget dollars for childcare so parents of younger children can participate in an evening of relationship-building. If the church leaders decide that having a trained teaching faculty is a "win," then they will budget enough dollars to train their group leaders.

3. **"Clarifying the win" helps you evaluate and adjust.** It's important for groups and group leaders to be able to accurately evaluate their progress in meeting assigned goals. Clarifying the win gives people a target. It helps them focus on the main things that are important. And it gives the pastor and staff the tools needed to evaluate groups and group leaders so they can make small adjustments in order to more fully meet the goals and objectives of the Sunday School.

STEPS FOR CLARIFYING THE WIN

A journey always starts with a single step. Here are some initial steps to "clarify the win" so that group leaders bring focus to the Sunday School ministry. Consider them the first steps on the journey to breathing new life into your Sunday School.

1. **Decide on what "winning" looks like in your Sunday School.** Compare this to your church's vision and mission statements. Pray. Involve key leaders. Find agreement. Keep it short. Make it memorable. People must be able to recall the essential things.

2. **Communicate what "winning" looks like every chance you get.** As you meet with Sunday School leaders, never meet without

reinforcing some or all of the things that constitute winning for your Sunday School. As you send out emails or tweets, talk about it there. Call attention to leaders who are "getting it" and succeeding in accomplishing the core actions that your team says are the most important. You'll feel like you're over-communicating this. You're not.

3. **"Clarify the win" through a teacher covenant.** A teacher covenant doesn't have to be long in order to be effective. A simple list of four to seven items can bring clarity and unity to your Sunday School. As new teachers are recruited and existing ones are re-enlisted, ask them to agree to a teacher covenant that clarifies the win. Ask them to sign it, commit to it, and help them by reviewing the elements several times a year to make sure they are on track.

Ask yourself if your church has effectively "clarified the win" for its Sunday School teachers. Do they know the essential, non-negotiable things they must accomplish each year? Are you regularly reminding them of what a "win" looks like? If you don't clarify the win, your leaders will clarify the win for themselves. And you may or may not like what they decide. So, tell them what you want. Be proactive. Be clear. Clarify.

HOW I CLARIFIED THE WIN

Years ago, I decided to "clarify the win" for my Sunday School leaders and I rebranded our Sunday School with the pastor's permission and blessing. I hope the story of our Sunday School might inspire your thinking. What our church did may not be right for your church, so don't run out and copy and paste our plan!

We changed the name of our Sunday School to LIFE Groups. This took place in 2004. I created an acrostic for the word LIFE that detailed the four key "wins" every group was to accomplish.

I had these four expectations turned into large posters that we mounted at the front of every classroom. Each week my group leaders and their group members were reminded of the four key "wins" that were expected.

Learn and apply God's Word

Invite others to become Christ followers

Form authentic relationships

Engage in service to others

We changed the name of Sunday School, but it was done with intentionality and not because we thought Sunday School was an out-of-date term. We simply wanted to define winning for our group leaders, group members, and guests. Let's unpack each of the four parts of the LIFE acrostic. These four things became the measuring sticks of success in our groups. This is how we clarified the win at my church.

Learn and apply God's Word. When people think about Sunday School, this is the one they most likely think about first. It's important for Christians to learn what the Bible says, who wrote the various books, and how the sixty-six books in our Bible connect to tell one larger story of man's redemption. But I don't want groups studying just to study. Knowledge is necessary, but it sometimes causes us to puff up with pride (1 Cor. 8:1). As groups of believers come together, this first "win" of Sunday School must extend into everyday life. It's one thing to learn information about the Bible. It is quite another thing to apply the Bible's teaching to life. But that's the goal. Jesus told His disciples to teach "them to obey" (Matt. 28:20, NIV). We teach in order to develop obedient disciples. We don't teach simply to teach information. Instead, we partner with the Holy Spirit and teach in such a way that people undergo spiritual transformation. Transformation trumps information.

Invite others to become Christ followers. Sunday School is a missionary movement. It began in England and was transplanted to the United States when the first colonists settled America. It spread West as the country expanded. The goal was to reach people for Christ, children in particular. An important aspect of Sunday School today should be evangelism. Too many groups have lost an evangelistic focus, and they've turned inward. It takes vigilance to keep Sunday School groups focused on reaching the lost. But that's what a key "win" is. It's about people taking seriously their responsibility to be evangelists. It's about our groups being open to reaching new people and having new Christians alongside maturing ones in a group.

It's about group leaders intentionally presenting the gospel as they teach. According to Arthur Flake, "In this work [teaching] lies the teacher's best opportunity to make his life tell for Jesus. He should have a complete prayer list of all the lost pupils in his class and daily spread this list out before God and claim his promise to save them. Each one of them by name should be presented at the throne of grace."[36]

Form authentic relationships. If you'd asked me twenty years ago what's important in a Sunday School group, I'd have quickly answered, "the teaching." My top spiritual gifts are teaching and knowledge. I love to study. I love to guide Bible study. But as I've matured over the years and have led a weekly Bible study group for the past five years, I'd respond differently to that question today. I have come to realize that people are hungry—maybe even starving—for authentic relationships. They want friends who genuinely care about them. They need that "two a.m. friend." And Sunday School groups can help people connect with others who become lifelong friends. In order to help people experience transformational relationships, I believe that small to mid-size groups are the best for fostering this. I have experienced this in my group that averages sixteen people in attendance. I have friends in education ministry who have declared that the optimal size for a group is twelve, plus or minus four. In my experience, that's about right. If groups get too large, group leaders turn into presenters, not guides. They cannot know people like they would if the group was smaller. They can't connect people to others in ways they can when groups are smaller. Disciples are made in smaller groups.

Engage in service to others. David Francis, former Sunday School Director at LifeWay, once said that the natural inertia of any group is to turn inward. It was a brilliant observation, and it's completely true. This final component of group life—engaging in service to others—helps groups maintain an outward focus. One Bible study group under my leadership took this fourth component so seriously that they decided to adopt women from the local women's shelter. They did this one lady at a time, and when she graduated the program designed to help her gain her financial independence, this Bible study group presented her with a car! They did this several times while I was on staff at the church. I couldn't have been more proud of a group of people. The husband-wife team who led this group, Steve and Jackie Humphrey, got it; they engaged in service to others and shared Christ in the process. But the outward focus of groups is not just designed to be a focus out to people in the community. Engaging in service to others also means that people should leave their adult Bible study groups and serve in the student and children's ministries of the church. We asked group members to serve in the worship ministry or as greeters. We encouraged men to consider whether or not God was calling them to be deacons. The people responded once we told them what the "win" was. This is why I'm such a fan of "clarifying the win." I've seen it do great things for a Sunday School.

REINFORCING THE WIN

It's one thing to decide what a win looks like in your Sunday School. It's another thing to communicate what winning looks like. And it's an entirely different thing to continually reinforce what winning looks like.

Whether or not you use the LIFE acrostic I once did or whether you use another phrase or acrostic, it's important to continually reinforce what winning looks like to your group leaders and to your group members.

1. **Reinforce from the pulpit.** Pastors have a unique opportunity to reinforce winning in the Sunday School. If you're a pastor, don't discount the influence you have. Focus your congregation's attention on the wins you want from the Sunday School. Whatever is important to a pastor becomes important to his church. Interview a group leader during the worship service from time to time or a family that has been impacted by Sunday School. Show your congregation real people who are benefiting from the ministry of the Sunday School.

2. **Reinforce during the new members class.** Many churches now offer or require potential members to attend a new members class. This is a good venue through which to introduce people to the expectations you have of the church's group ministry. Having done this in the past, I can tell you that it raised the attendance and participation levels in my church's Sunday School. We simply explained what winning was for the Sunday School, and the people responded.

3. **Reinforce during training.** Every time you gather together to train your group leaders, something should be said to drive home the wins you want from your groups. Talk about them. Focus on them. Reward them. Show your leaders what winning looks like. When you see a group or a group leader succeeding in accomplishing one of your values, brag on that group and that group leader in front of others. People repeat what is rewarded, so find creative ways to reward the behavior you're trying to modify.

4. **Reinforce in ongoing communication.** As you tweet, send letters, write emails, develop your website, and have conversations, learn to infuse those things with comments, stories, and reminders about the wins that are taking place in your Sunday School. You're going to feel like you're talking about it too much, but remember it takes people a while to hear the message, believe the message, and act on the message. And you always have new people coming into the congregation who haven't heard what winning looks like. You'll think you are over-communicating, but you won't be.

5. **Reinforce through budgeting.** An excellent way to reinforce the wins you want in your Sunday School is to set up your annual budget in categories that support the wins you've declared you want. Take me for example. If I were using my LIFE acrostic today in the church, I could easily budget around the four wins I wanted to see taking place. The first category would be "Learning and applying God's Word." Underneath that heading, I would budget for curriculum, classroom supplies, children's toys and learning objects, electronics, Bibles, and anything else that helps me and my group leaders guide people of all ages to study and apply the Bible. In the next category, I'd budget for "Invite others to become Christ followers." That's the second of the four wins I wanted. I would budget for evangelism training, outreach events sponsored by Sunday School groups, and other things that help groups and group leaders share the gospel. You get the idea. The budgeting process and the way the budget is framed can help you reinforce the wins you desire from your groups.

FOR FURTHER THOUGHT

1. In what ways have you "clarified the win" for your group leaders? How would you judge the effectiveness?

2. If you haven't clarified the win at your church, who should be involved in that conversation? List their names here.

3. If you clarified the win with your group leaders, how might that change your Sunday School?

4. Clarify the win right now. Use the space below to jot down the key things that you would consider a "win" if the groups at your church accomplished them.

07

ESSENTIAL 7: DOWNSIZE FOR DISCIPLESHIP

There is a tourist destination in southwest Kentucky. It's not too far from my home in the Nashville area. The Corvette® Museum is located in Bowling Green, Kentucky, and you can see lots of Corvettes. There are interactive exhibits, and you can learn a lot about the history of the Corvette automobile. You can also take a tour of the Corvette factory next door.

It's amazing to watch the assembly of Corvettes at the factory. In fact, in the time I stood there to watch the process, not one Ford® rolled off the production line. Neither did any Nissan.® Conspicuously absent were other kinds of Chevrolets.® The only vehicles that emerged at the end of the production process was, you guessed it, Corvettes.

The entire factory is designed to produce one type of vehicle. The workers are trained to produce one kind of car, the Corvette. Everything about this factory lines up with its mission to make Corvettes. The church is like this Corvette factory in a way. The church takes in raw materials: people. It has processes in place to take those people and produce one thing: disciples.

What might happen if we aligned the church's mission of making disciples with the one organization that has the majority of our people in it? Churches are beginning to rediscover that Sunday School is foundational discipleship. The mission of Sunday School is to produce one thing: disciples. And it's propelled along when disciples are made in smaller groups.

Jesus discipled twelve men but also had a "group within a group." He spent time with Peter, James, and John—His inner circle of disciples—and poured into their lives in ways He did not do with the others. This does not discount the importance of preaching the Word, but it acknowledges that preaching plus disciple-making in smaller groups is a powerful combination.

SMALLER IS BETTER

Preaching to large crowds is fun. Teaching large groups is equally energizing. But if this was Jesus' plan for making disciples, wouldn't we find Him teaching in coliseums, amphitheaters, and other venues where hundreds or even thousands of people could gather at one time? It appears that His primary method for making disciples centered around small groups. His group of twelve disciples and His inner group of three disciples, was foundational to His plan to create the first disciples who would lead His church.

The authors of *Transformational Groups*, Ed Stetzer and Eric Geiger, spoke to the present-day need for churches to reconsider the biblical model for making disciples. They said, "So many churches are trying to get larger... The church needs to make getting smaller a priority...We want people gathered in worship, then in smaller groups."[37] If you want to breathe new life into Sunday School, downsize your largest groups to make disciples. In some churches, groups have gotten much too large to effectively make disciples.

In 1930, LifeWay's first Director of Sunday School, Arthur Flake, wrote about the need to downsize groups. We've known for years that the most effective way to make disciples is in smaller groups! He said, "Even at their best, large Sunday School classes of adults and young people with attractive orators as teachers will never function effectively in teaching the Bible. Until these large classes have been replaced by small groups of not more than ten to fifteen young people, and ten to twenty-five adults, and until sharing learning activities replaces lecturing as the main method of teaching, there will never be the most effective Bible learning by the rank and file of members of the young people's and adult departments."[38]

I recently spoke to education and discipleship leaders in different parts of the country. In the past thirty days, I had conversations with church leaders in Kansas, Texas, and Oklahoma. The common denominator? These three leaders from three very different churches spoke of the large 100-person classes in their churches. Their teachers teach in large lecture halls. Some groups have almost 150 people in them—which is more people than the average Southern Baptist church! While I'm sure teaching is taking place, I have to wonder how disciples are being made in such lecture-driven environments in which participation during the study is so low.

WHAT IS A DISCIPLE?

I've read approximately twenty books on discipleship over the past two years. I have several professors in my doctoral program to thank for exposing me to thought leaders in the field of discipleship. One of my favorite authors, Aubrey Malphurs, defines a disciple this way: "A disciple is one who has trusted in Christ as Savior. In short, he or she is a believer in Christ…a disciple may be a deeply committed believer who is 'sold out' to Christ; however, a disciple may also not be a committed believer, but still a believer in Christ. Committed disciples are committed believers, and uncommitted disciples are uncommitted believers. What both have in common is that they share a faith in Christ as Savior."[39]

To say it another way, saved people are disciples. Some are more mature than others, but all Christians are disciples. That's the way the New Testament presents them. These new disciples are best served by being placed in a smaller group of fellow disciples where they can know people and be known by them. Fledgling disciples need the nurture and support of other believers. They need friends. They need a job to do. They need to relate to more mature believers who can help them on their journey.

IMPLICATIONS OF DISCIPLE MAKING FOR SUNDAY SCHOOL GROUPS

I taught a Sunday School group at my church, and now I'm asking myself the question, "Did I really make disciples through my ministry as a teacher?" This question has haunted me lately. I don't want to teach my group members lots of interesting biblical facts so I can hear them "ooh" and "ahh" when I tell them something they've not previously heard. I want to be obedient to Jesus' command to "go and make disciples." How about you? Making disciples involves teaching them, but before I can teach them, I must evangelize them. And I must keep my group's focus outward; we must be reminded often that we exist to reach people who are far from God.

It's my observation that in some places, Sunday School has accidentally morphed into an information-dispensing ministry with very large groups. While I know that people need information about the Bible, that cannot be the end game. The real goal of Sunday School is to make disciples. Making disciples involves more than just teaching facts. Making disciples starts with evangelism. Making disciples means placing people in small groups so they can grow.

SMALLER GROUPS FOCUS ON EVANGELISM AND OUTREACH

One of the most frustrating things I hear from time to time is, "Sunday School isn't deep enough." Maybe someone has said that to you, too. Some people believe that disciples need depth, and the Sunday School is the best place to take a deeper dive into Scripture. People seek out only the best teachers. Large groups get larger. Gifted teacher-communicators end up with large lecture classes. Such was the case with a woman who called me one day.

She called to express her displeasure that the Sunday School curriculum being studied by her group just wasn't deep enough for her group of senior adult ladies. They are a large group of women who have combined several classes over the years to form one "mega class."

"My group is well beyond the content of the materials," she said. "I attend two other in-depth Bible studies each week, and the Sunday School materials need to be more like those. Those other studies are challenging, and they require lots of hours of homework. We get into the meaning of the original languages. Sunday School materials need to be more like that."

I quickly gathered my thoughts and I asked her, "Ma'am, how many lost people do you have in your Sunday School class?" There was silence on the other end of the line, and then she said, "None I know of." I followed up with, "What about new believers? How many of those kinds of people are in your group?" Again, she said, "None."

I explained to her that this is the real problem, not the curriculum. I could tell she had never stopped to consider this.

I told her that Sunday School is foundational discipleship. It's designed to have open groups that use ongoing curriculum. It's designed to reach people with the gospel. It's supposed to help make disciples, and that starts when people are introduced to the Bible and to the One who authored it.

This dear sister didn't know what an open group was. I explained that open groups expect new people to be there every week. They hope and pray for that. Lost adults are likely to be found sitting next to believers who are maturing in their faith, which is a very good thing.

Open groups also use ongoing Bible study materials. Each session stands on its own. It's designed to be a complete and satisfying Bible study experience. Even though it may connect to the study before and after it, a person doesn't have to experience those in order for the current session to make sense.

The lady finally understood the real problem. She expected Sunday School to be the place for deeper discipleship. She was perfectly comfortable with her group being turned inward. She was content even though there were no lost people in her group. She'd either forgotten or never been taught the real mission of Sunday School: to make disciples. That means groups should have people in them who are far from God alongside growing, maturing believers.

Sunday School is about pre-Christians engaging in Bible study with maturing believers. I would wish that every Sunday School group would have a healthy mixture of Christians and non-Christians. Sadly, this isn't so. Arthur Flake has said, "The supreme business of Christianity is to win the lost to Christ. This is what churches are for. It was Christ's one supreme mission, according to his own words. 'For the Son of man is come to seek and to save that which was lost' (Luke 19:10)…Surely then the Sunday School must relate itself to the winning of the lost to Christ as an ultimate objective."[40]

Disciples follow. Disciples sacrifice. Disciples obey. Disciples commit. Disciples learn. Disciples serve. Disciples lead. Disciples grow…sometimes beyond their teachers.

Does this describe the average person in your group? In your Sunday School? If not, perhaps it's time to rethink why your Sunday School, or your group, exists.

Robby Gallaty, pastor and author of *Growing Up: How to Be a Disciple Who Makes Disciples*, says, "When the church becomes an end in itself, it ends. When Sunday School, as great as it is, becomes an end in itself, it ends. When small groups ministry becomes an end in itself, it ends. When the worship service becomes an end in itself, it ends. What we need is for discipleship to become the goal, and then the process never ends. The process is fluid. It is moving. It is active. It is a living thing. It must continue to go on. Every disciple must make disciples."[41]

To make disciples through a Sunday School ministry, at least three things need to happen. These are a starting point for creating disciples through your church's Sunday School ministry:

1. **Groups must downsize.** Discipleship happens when small groups of people come together. Jesus' model for making disciples seems to include two primary groups: (1) a group of three (often referred to as "His inner circle" of disciples) and (2) the twelve disciples. It's true He sometimes spoke to very large crowds (Sermon on the Mount, in the temple courtyards, etc.), but His normal way to make disciples was to do so in small groups. This has the advantage of allowing the leader to know his learners and what each one needs in order to grow and become more Christlike.

2. **Group leaders must let others talk.** Disciple-making teachers know that people need to be allowed to talk and encouraged to talk, at least as much as they do. For some group leaders, this is counter-intuitive. Somewhere along the way, many teachers have adopted a mentality that says, "I'm the expert, and you're not, so listen to what I have to say." It's true that teachers often study for many hours in preparation to teach their group members, and that is highly commendable and appropriate. But what's truly effective in a group Bible study is when teachers become guides who lead their people to discuss biblical truths, wrestle with truths presented in Scripture, and challenge assumptions and actions. Without that, the class ends up being a place in which a monologue takes place weekly.

3. **Churches must answer the "why" question.** Before discipleship can take place through the Sunday School, it's helpful and necessary for

church leaders, group leaders, and group members to wrestle with the reason Sunday School exists in the first place. Sunday School is an expression of our obedience to the Great Commission. Fellowship, Bible study, ministry, and outreach are all part of what Sunday School seeks to accomplish, but they are not an end in themselves. The real goal of Sunday School should be to see disciples made. That's really why Sunday school exists in the first place. We must constantly be on guard for "discipleship drift." I'm glad when groups study. I'm equally glad when groups have fun together and pray together. But I'm elated when I see groups reaching new people and making disciples. That's the mission.

Jim Putman and Bobby Harrington, in their book, *DiscipleShift: 5 Steps That Help Your Church To Make Disciples*, say, "We believe...a church should make an intentional shift that nurtures the type of biblical relational discipleship we have been talking about. Since making disciples is the main reason why a church exists, everything in the corporate body of the local church needs to be aligned in a way that funnels people toward these discipleship environments, the most notable of which is the relational small group."[42]

Note their emphasis on small. That's the key.

WHY DOWNSIZED GROUPS ARE BETTER

What's the ideal size for a Bible study group? I'd like to follow the advice of David Francis and Rick Howerton suggested in their book, *Countdown*, that a group of twelve, plus or minus four, is about the right size.[43] David has long been recognized as an expert in Sunday School; Rick is recognized as a small-group expert. Both agree that smaller is better. If you want to make disciples through your Sunday School, here are some reasons why groups should downsize.

1. **Downsized groups can meet anywhere.** A group of twelve people (which I would consider to be "about the right size," give or take a few) can meet in any on-campus room at the church, and they can fit comfortably in someone's living room. They can also fit around the table at a coffee shop or restaurant.

2. **Downsized groups increase conversational community**. People in a large class tend to remain quiet. Speaking up in front of a group of forty or fifty peers can be very intimidating, so some really great comments always go unspoken. In a smaller group, the intimidation factor doesn't exist like it does in a large group. As Dr. Ed Stetzer, former president of LifeWay Research, said in his book *Transformational Groups*, "A small group or class Bible study should be a 'groupalogue.' A groupalogue is a study built on great questions…Your effectiveness goes up incredibly as does learning when everyone is talking…"[44]

3. **Downsized groups help people connect.** People have only so many relationships they can give their time, attention, and energy to supporting. Each of us has only so many connections we can make (and keep). Smaller groups tend to help people connect with one another and form relationships. It's simply easier to make friends in smaller groups.

4. **Downsized groups are less intimidating to lead.** Have you ever tried to recruit someone to teach a large "pastor's class"? It takes a special person with special biblical knowledge to teach such a large group of people. When that person steps down, moves away, retires, etc., finding a replacement can be just about impossible. In smaller groups, leaders are much easier to recruit. Guiding the Bible study of a group of twelve is much easier than trying to teach a large class.

5. **Downsized groups keep people from falling through cracks**. One of the jobs of a group leader is to act as a shepherd for their group. To read more about this, pick up a copy of the book *3 Roles for Guiding Groups*. In this book, David Francis and I spend an entire chapter on the role of shepherd, and how a good teacher-shepherd knows his sheep, keeps up with them, prays for them, and watches over them.[45] It's physically impossible to do this in a large classroom setting with dozens and dozens of people in the group. I teach a group of sixteen adults weekly at my church, and between my full-time job, my role as a husband and father, and other responsibilities, it's all I can do to minister to this smaller group of adults! I can't imagine trying to teach and shepherd a group of thirty, forty, or fifty adults.

6. **Downsized groups are places where discipleship takes place.** Jesus taught and ministered to large groups, but His favorite method for making disciples was investing in twelve disciples, not 100 disciples. Even within His group of twelve there was an "inner group" of three men with whom He spent even more relational time. Jesus' model was to use a small group as the basis for discipleship. Somewhere along the way, we've gotten away from this biblical example. A teacher who disciples his people knows each of them, their needs, their shortcomings, and what each one needs to progress in their journey toward Christlikeness. In a large lecture-oriented class, I might make a good presentation, but I won't generate much conversation and I certainly won't see as much transformation as I might when I lead and disciple a smaller group of adults.

Robby Gallaty recounted a conversation with Avery Willis who perhaps said it best, "Preaching to make disciples is like going to the nursery and spraying the crying babies with milk and saying you just fed the kids… discipleship involves more than preaching and listening."[46] Preaching is a good thing, but large groups are not the best place for making disciples. Large Sunday School classes aren't the right place, either.

If you want to breathe life into your Sunday School, you're going to want to downsize in order to make disciples.

FOR FURTHER THOUGHT

1. Think about the average size group in your Sunday School. Is it somewhere between the size of eight to sixteen people? How many is it?

2. In what ways does Sunday School serve as a place for foundational discipleship?

3. What can you do in order to help people connect the mission of the Sunday School with the biblical mandate to make disciples?

4. Which of the benefits of having downsized groups would be most attractive to your church right now? Why?

ESSENTIAL 8: ENROLL YOUR GUESTS

Before I enrolled for college and seminary courses, I was unknown to those schools. I lived in the community where the schools were located, but I was not in their computer system nor on any mailing lists. They didn't know I existed. It was only when I enrolled to take classes that my name was placed on a professor's class list, and I was given a syllabus and assigned reading and homework, among other things. Enrolling in college meant that a professor became responsible for me. I was now part of the system.

Guests visit our churches and our Bible study groups each week. They are unknown to us until they give us their contact information. When a guest visits a Bible study group, one of the first things we must do is invite them to enroll and become part of the group. There should be a clear understanding they are not committing to join the church. They are simply connecting with a Bible study group. As a member of a group, they'll be cared for. They'll be invited to group parties. They'll have opportunities to serve. They'll be lifted up in prayer.

Enrollment leads to connection. Connection often leads to membership. "The picture is clear: people stick to a church when they get involved in a small group...When people move to a group, they are known. They are able to live life with other people...they stick. They stay. They last. They have a support network, a community of fellow Christ followers."[47] Enrolling people in a group is an important step toward solidifying a person's connection to the church.

Unfortunately, some churches have rules that work against enrolling people the first time they visit a group. "Visit three times in a row and then we can enroll you," one church's policy says. In other churches, group leaders simply don't ask guests to enroll. People need help taking the next steps toward church membership. Belonging to a Bible study group helps them take a big step toward church membership. Allan Taylor has said, "We should be constantly enrolling new Sunday School members. We want everyone participating in Bible study…we must see Sunday School as an 'open door' organization and not a 'closed door' society."[48]

REDISCOVERING ENROLLMENT

Enrolling people in Bible study is a visible indicator that a church or Bible study group is seeking to obey The Great Commission. Deuteronomy 31:12, John 17:18-21, Galatians 1:16, and of course Matthew 28:19-20, all demonstrate the necessity of reaching people with the gospel, and of the need for instructing them in God's Word.

One of my heroes in Christian education, Dr. Harry Piland, wrote about this in his book, *Basic Sunday School Work*. The emphasis on the word "basic" here—there is nothing new and innovative about reaching out to people and enrolling them in Bible study. It's something we must rediscover today. In his book, Dr. Piland made the following observation. "One of the best ways to reach out and touch this vast unreached population is to get people involved in Bible study. We can do so by enrolling them in Sunday School…To reach means to enlist and involve persons in Bible study. It means enlisting and involving unsaved persons, unchurched Christians, members of a church who are not part of the Bible teaching program, and children of these groups."[49]

During Dr. Piland's tenure at LifeWay Christian Resources as Director of the Sunday School division, enrollment in Sunday School "increased from 7.3 million to 8.2 million."[50] Enrolling people in Bible study was a passion for Dr. Piland, and he knew it was essential for breathing life into Sunday School. If you want your Sunday School to grow, you must enroll new people in Bible study groups.

OPEN GROUPS AND OPEN ENROLLMENT

There are ten common factors in fast-growing Sunday School churches. Research has demonstrated that 91% of churches that are fast-growing practice open enrollment, meaning that anyone can join a Bible study group anywhere, at any time.[51] The groups are open to new people. The fast-growing Sunday School churches have learned an important truth. Enrolling new people leads to growth in attendance.

I've always followed the practice that you should ask a person to enroll in a group the first time they visit. Once on a group's ministry role, the group leader becomes responsible for being that new enrollee's teacher-shepherd.

Enrollment increases accountability. Accountability leads to better ministry. Better ministry leads to a healthier Sunday School and a healthier church. It's all connected.

The best Sunday Schools are intentionally designed to have open groups. An open group is one that assumes a new person (or persons) may be in attendance each time the group meets. An open group expects new people to be present. Because of this anticipation, members of open groups wear name tags, they use ongoing Bible study materials and have extra copies for guests, there are empty chairs for guests, and the group has greeters who welcome guests and help them meet others.

THE CONNECTION BETWEEN ENROLLMENT AND ATTENDANCE

Teacher "A" is content with his class of ten people. Teacher "B" has the same size group but wants to grow and reach more people for Christ. He's hoping to involve people that do not currently belong to a Bible study group.

Now that Teacher "B" has decided he wants the group to grow, how would you advise him to go about increasing attendance? There is a tried and true way to do just that, and it's easier than you might think. You can do this with an entire Sunday School or small group ministry.

First, we must realize that enrollment and attendance are inseparable. One is influenced by the other. They are two sides of the same coin. Let me explain.

Attendance is almost always 45-50% of a group's enrollment. Teacher "B" and Teacher "A" have ten people who are regular attenders in their groups. That means that each one has about twenty people on a ministry role.

Teacher "B" needs to lead his group to enroll new people. Open enrollment can happen (1) any time and (2) anywhere. Every guest should be asked to enroll in the group. The guests need to know that enrolling in the Bible study doesn't mean they are committing to join the church. They are simply taking a step into group life by aligning themselves with a leader and his group. They are giving the group permission to care about them.

If Teacher "B" enrolls ten new people, he can anticipate his average attendance rising to about fifteen (enroll ten and five will attend on average). If Teacher "B" wants to grow the group again, he and his group can be intentional about enrolling even more new people. It's that simple. Once on a ministry roll, a person has a higher probability of being contacted, prayed for, and encouraged to attend the Bible study.

Enrolling the person is important. Following up with the person and helping him belong to the group is also important. The two must be done together. It's not enough to enroll someone and expect the group to grow.

WHAT ABOUT YOUR CHURCH?

Let's say that a church's Sunday School or small group ministry had a goal of growing 100 people during the upcoming year. What would they need to do? It's simple: enroll 200 new people to see average attendance rise by 100. In this example, the church's Sunday School would need to enroll 3.84 people per week. That's one family. Or it's one preschooler, one child, one student, and one adult. Or it's four adults. Or two students and two adults. You get the picture. It's achievable. It's just under four people per week.

I've done some math for you in the table below. Take a look and see which scenario best describes your desired increase in attendance.

DESIRED INCREASE IN SUNDAY SCHOOL ATTENDANCE	NEW ENROLLEES NEEDED	NEW ENROLLEES PER MONTH	NEW ENROLLEES PER WEEK
25	50	2.08	.48
50	100	4.16	.96
100	200	8.33	1.9
150	300	12.5	2.8
200	400	16.7	3.8
250	500	20.8	4.8

What we're really talking about in this example are lead and lag measures. A lead measure is something you set as your target goal. If you hit the lead measure, a certain result follows (the lag measure).

For instance, if I wanted to lose weight, I could set lead measures of walking five miles a day and reducing my caloric intake each day. The lag measure would be my weight, which presumably would be headed downward if I achieved my lead measures of exercise and diet.

In the world of Sunday School, lead and lag measures work the same way. We set up-front goals, and results lag behind. Lead and lag measures create a weekly scorecard on which you can track your progress. It's all about bringing accountability to the organization. You can check each week to see whether or not you're hitting your lead metrics with regard to enrollment.

TAKING ENROLLMENT GOALS TO THE NEXT LEVEL

If my Sunday School averaged 200 people per week, and I wanted to set a goal of averaging 250 people one year from now, the Sunday School must enroll at least 100 new people. 100 new enrollees would give the Sunday School an increase of about 50 people in groups (remember, attendance is almost always 50% of enrollment).

In this current 100-person example, those 100 new enrollees will come from all age groups, right? So how many preschoolers, children, students, and adults should you enroll to achieve your 100-person enrollment goal?

The answer lies in your current attendance patterns.

Every church has a pattern of attendance in their Sunday School. Gather your Sunday School attendance records and determine the average attendance year-to-date.

Once you determine the average attendance of your Sunday School, then discover what percent of that number are preschool, children, student, and adults on any given Sunday.

Let's say that you do the math and determine that on any given Sunday, your preschool attendance is 10% of your total attendance, children are 20% of your total attendance, students are 20% of your total attendance, and adults are 50% of your total attendance. These figures won't change much over time unless something very dramatic happens in your church.

Now, let's go back to the challenge of enrolling 100 new people this year. 10% of those new enrollees should be preschoolers (10), 20% should be children (20), another 20% will be students (20), and 50 will be adults (50%). Now you can set enrollment goals for each age division and follow up each week to see whether or not they are meeting the enrollment goals. Looking at enrollment goals like this simply creates a cadence of accountability in each age division. It's also a fair way to assign accountability. If adults were 25% of the total attendance, it wouldn't be fair to ask that age division to enroll 50% of the new enrollees.

One final word of encouragement: in the example above of enrolling 100 new people, you'd only have to enroll one new preschooler each month (.83 actually!) in order to achieve your enrollment goal for that area of ministry. You'd have to enroll 1.6 children each month (the same for students since they are both 20% of your attendance on any given Sunday) and 4.16 adults per month (or about one adult per week)! When you break enrollment goals down, you'll discover how manageable they really are. One hundred new enrollees may seem daunting, but remember the saying, "It's a cinch by the inch; it's hard by the yard." And I know you know how to eat an elephant: one bite at a time. Enrollment goals help you eat the elephant in small enough bites that you can experience success.

DON'T FORGET THIS

One caveat about all of this. It's one thing to set enrollment and attendance goals, but don't forget that the people you enroll must have space, curriculum, a group to which they can belong, a teacher, and a group that is open. You must manage all of these things simultaneously. If you don't, it won't matter how many people you enroll.

Plus, you must manage the enrollment and growth in each age division simultaneously. If one ministry area runs out of space or gets stalled out, it will affect the other three ministry areas. If enrollment goals are met in the adult division, but there's a lack of teachers and space in the preschool ministry, younger parents will not trust the church with their children. The church will hit its enrollment goals, but because it doesn't have adequate space to receive new preschoolers, the parents won't attend.

FOR FURTHER THOUGHT

1. What adjustments would your Sunday School need to make in order for every age division to grow together?

2. What attendance/enrollment goal is reasonable and achievable by the groups at your church? How quickly do you believe your Sunday School can enroll the number of people required to raise your actual attendance to the point you desire?

3. What would you say to a group leader who is not enthusiastic about enrolling new people with intentionality the first time they visit the Bible study group?

4. What is your biggest take away from this chapter?

09

ESSENTIAL 9: KNOW KEY NUMBERS

In 2001, Oakland A's manager Billy Beane attempted to field a competitive team of players on a very limited budget. He and his staff analyzed computer-generated metrics of players and assembled the team based on those key numbers. Billy Beane and his staff paid attention to key numbers that other teams overlooked. They knew their key numbers.[52]

Sabermetrics, the process of evaluating player potential based on their on-base percentage, was a different approach than the traditional method of scouting players and basing decisions on intuition and other factors. The Oakland A's were able to acquire players with the right metrics, and although they did not advance to the World Series that season, the Red Sox won it two years later (2004) using the sabermetric approach.[53] It changed baseball forever.

As Sunday School leaders, we would be wise to pay attention to key metrics, too. Numbers matter.

Bible study groups have numerous things that impact their ability to grow, assimilate people, and make disciples. Here are important numbers you must know and respond to if you want to give your groups the best opportunity to grow. The following numbers are in no particular order, but they are all important and impact your ability to grow the Bible teaching ministry of your church. If you pay attention to the following numbers, you'll be well on your way to breathing life into your Sunday School.

24

The average ongoing Bible study group tends to calcify after the members have been together for twenty-four months or longer. I actually believe that groups may calcify a little earlier than this, perhaps around the 18-month mark. Although the relationships formed among group members tend to be strong, they can also be barriers when guests try to join the group. Groups and group leaders would do themselves (and potential new members) a favor by encouraging the formation of new groups from existing ones so that guests can connect with others relationally. It's much easier to assimilate into a newer group than an older, established group.

We've discussed the importance of starting new groups in an earlier chapter, so I won't go back over that now. Let this serve as a reminder of the important need for continually starting new groups so that guests don't "bounce off" of your existing groups. People enjoy studying the Bible together, but don't kid yourself about the important desire many have to make new friends and feel the support of a group.

15

Adults need space, and fifteen square feet per person is the recommended amount of space per adult so that the meeting space doesn't begin to feel claustrophobic. Take the group I used to teach, for example. I led a group of sixteen adults to study the Bible weekly. According to this formula, I should have had a minimum of 240 square feet in the place we met. As it turns out, I had just slightly more than the recommended 240 square feet, but not much more! While I did have room for the group members to meet, the chances of growing the group significantly beyond the average attendance of sixteen adults was minimal. My only two choices would have been to move to a larger meeting place, or I could have led my group to start another one. The latter is always the better of the two choices.

1

Every ongoing Bible study group needs prospects. You can keep a list electronically or do it the old-fashioned way with paper and pen, but groups must have prospects. It is recommended that groups have one prospect for every member of the group in attendance. Let's go back to my example above. My group of sixteen adults should have had a minimum of sixteen prospects at all times. Groups need a pool of prospects because they're going to lose people over time. Some people will move out of the city, possibly move to a different group within the church, experience a job relocation, die, etc. Every group has attrition. If I don't have enough prospects I'm encouraging to be part of my group, then I will see a decline in attendance over time.

During my college days I worked for the JCPenney® company. For several years I sold men's clothing on commission, and the big reason for my success was the way I worked my prospect file. I was religious about asking every person who purchased something from me to fill out a short form with their basic information on it. It went into my prospect file, and every time we had a sale, I sent out hundreds of letters and postcards in the weeks leading up to the sale. People came in to see me, not other salespersons, and I watched my income grow. It paid for my college and seminary courses, and I won some valuable prizes along the way.

Prospecting (that's what we called the process of maintaining a file and making contact regularly with prospects) is something I've learned is important when it comes to helping Bible study groups grow.

One reason that Bible study groups don't grow is because the group doesn't maintain a prospect file. In his book, *The Bonsai Theory of Church Growth*, Dr. Ken Hemphill suggests that groups have one prospect for every member.[54] Do you know how many prospects your church has on file? If you are a group leader, do you have a prospect file? If not, it's time to get a file!

HOW MANY PROSPECTS DO GROUPS HAVE, REALLY?

Church growth experts say that each of us know at least five people who are not involved in a small group. If an existing Bible study group has ten people on average, then all together the group knows fifty people who are potential prospects. All the group would have to do is collect the information about those people (names, addresses, emails, etc.) and begin contacting them regularly. That's how prospecting works.

LifeWay Research has indicated that one third of unchurched adults would attend a worship service if they were invited.[55] In the example above, if a group of ten knows fifty prospects, and if one third would attend if invited, then the group has the potential to grow by sixteen to seventeen people! That's good growth.

When Tammy and I launched our new Bible study group years ago, the church provided a list of forty nine prospects (often called a "paper" class since it is a listing of potential group members). We sent out letters and emails. We made a series of phone calls. We prospected. On our first day, six people came to the Bible study to check it out. We continued to work the prospect list, and the group ultimately grew to about sixteen adults present each week.

If you are a pastor or staff leader, perhaps you should lead your groups to create prospect files. If you are a group leader, create a prospect file (electronic or paper) and send out regular invitations to your group's fellowships, meals, and oh yes, Bible study. Many prospects will resonate with invitations to parties, and they actually become part of your group before becoming an official part of your group. Others will be attracted to a Bible study topic you're studying. The bottom line is this: if you aren't prospecting on a regular basis and keeping an active prospect file, your group may decline over time because people move away, stop attending, etc. The possibility of growing your group can be tied to how aggressive you are in reaching out to prospects. If your Bible study groups maintain active prospect files, you'll see your attendance rise. The Sunday School will experience improved health.

48

Studies have proven that the faster a group reaches out to guests, a higher percentage of them return the following week. Groups should have a goal of contacting all guests within the first forty-eight hours of the visit. When follow-up after the initial visit doesn't happen quickly, the likelihood the person will return for a second visit decreases significantly. This should be a wake-up call to groups and group leaders. This is something they can improve upon. A reasonable goal would be to contact every guest within the first twenty-four hours after their initial visit, but certainly no later than forty-eight hours after their visit.

One church my wife and I visited came by our house to return the visit on Sunday afternoon immediately following the worship service. My family had eaten at a restaurant on the way home from church that day, only to find a gift bag and note on our front porch. This particular church had a plan in place to visit each guest right after church. From a potential new member's perspective, I have to say this was very impressive! We felt valued, welcomed, and important.

10

Every new group that is properly started grows the Sunday School ministry by ten people on average. When I launched my Bible study group a few years ago, it started out by reaching a small handful of people. As time went by, attendance grew to an average of sixteen. I've experienced the truism that new groups reach ten people on average. Most end up reaching more. If a church desired to grow its Bible study ministry by fifty people in one year, it would start by launching at least five new groups. To make certain that it had a net growth of fifty people, it would probably need to start an additional group or two for a total of seven new groups to account for "churn," the decrease that takes place as people leave the church over the course of the year.

18

People take an average of eighteen months to join a church today.[56] I had a hard time believing this number until my family and I moved to a new city and experienced firsthand the challenges of finding a new church and a new Bible study group. My family took twelve months to find the church we believed God was leading us to join. I didn't anticipate it taking up to one year for our family to find a new church home. Because people are taking longer to join these days, diligence and consistent follow-up are key to helping guests connect with your church and a Bible study group. Groups must continue to reach out to guests who once visited them. It would be a mistake for groups to assume that people who have not joined are no longer interested. The truth is, they are simply taking their time. They're not in a rush.

1

Every member of each Bible study group needs their own copy of a PSG (Personal Study Guide). Some churches, in an attempt to save money, have either eliminated Personal Study Guides altogether or have cut back their orders, giving couples only one Personal Study Guide to share. In my 20+ years of education ministry leadership in the local church, I always provided one Personal Study Guide per person. By providing one Personal Study Guide per person, a church sends a signal that individual Bible study is important, and group leaders can use the Personal Study Guide in class to engage their members in active Bible study. It also communicates to the church and its guests that the church staff has a wise plan for discipling the people. When Personal Study Guides are not used in a group, we unintentionally communicate the message that we have a haphazard approach to selecting topics and Scripture passages to study. Instead, providing a Personal Study Guide communicates that groups are following a wisely chosen scope and sequence (the topics covered and the order in which they are studied), giving balance over time to "the whole counsel of God."

20

Churches should order extra PSGs (Personal Study Guides) for the guests who will come to Bible study groups over the course of several months. Additional PSGs (20% beyond the group's average attendance) are needed. This makes sure that guests can fully participate in the group experience, and it helps all group members and guests study and prepare to participate in upcoming studies. A church that orders 20% more PSGs is well-prepared to help guests feel like they are expected and wanted. My wife and I have visited groups where additional PSGs were not available, and we felt like outsiders who temporarily listened in on the regular attender's conversations about information in their PSGs. It's not a good feeling!

13,000

Every church has a per capita level of financial giving. You divide the weekly offering by the number of people in Sunday School or worship, and you arrive at a per capita level of giving for your church. If your church has a per capita of $25, and you add one new Bible study group, the church can anticipate adding $13,000 to its annual budget receipts. Ten people (which is the average increase in attendance caused by adding a new group) multiplied by $25 per capita equals $250 per week in tithes and offerings. $250 per week multiplied by fifty-two weeks equals $13,000 annually. The per capita giving of some churches is $50 or more. If that is the case, then one new Bible study group could benefit the church in the amount of about $26,000 per year in additional tithes and offerings.

35

I once surveyed hundreds of group leaders and church staff leaders regarding how much actual teaching time group leaders really have. I discovered that the average group has thirty-five minutes in which the members are engaged in a study of the Scripture. That's not a lot of time, so group leaders must be extremely focused when it comes time for them to guide the group's study.

If a group leader spends five minutes opening the group's study time (a time for the group leader to generate interest in the study) and five to ten minutes closing the study (helping group members connect the study to life today), that only leaves twenty to twenty-five minutes of actual teaching time. If a group leader has crafted three to four well-thought-out discussion questions (or used great questions provided in the teaching plans of his or her curriculum), those will take the group at least fifteen minutes to discuss.

That only leaves ten minutes in the group time during which the teacher must say things. The trap many group leaders fall into is talking the entire time, monopolizing the time group members could be discussing key points in the Bible study, sharing stories, and working through their understanding of the biblical text. Too many Bible study groups expect the teacher to be the expert, and some teachers take on that role, believing they must be the ones who study and prepare and then do what I call "an information dump." I'd much rather see a group leader use the thirty-five minutes to guide discovery—helping group members actively engage in the learning process. It's better for everyone, and group members will remember more of the biblical text and application points if they are allowed to discuss, struggle with, and seek to apply the Scriptures.

3

There are three essential stages to any good Bible study. The three stages are (1) motivation (2) examination (3) application. Think of this like a three-stage rocket seeking to escape the earth's gravity. Each stage provides thrust and momentum for the group study.

During the motivation stage, group leaders must capture the interest and attention of group members, guiding them to study the Scripture.

The examination stage is the time spent examining the Scripture passage. It includes the things the group leader says, and the things the group members do.

The final stage of study is the application stage—where group leaders help group members think through and commit to apply the lesson to their lives. Group leaders who have a balanced approach to their Bible study time, and who incorporate all three of these essential stages, help their groups grow by providing sound, interesting, and balanced studies that fully engage group members and give them practical ways to live out the Bible's teachings.

50

Fifty percent of group members are in attendance on almost any given occasion that groups come together for Bible study. A group with an average attendance of fifteen most likely has thirty people on the group's membership list. A group that averages thirty in attendance probably has sixty people on its ministry list, perhaps a few more.

This has two implications: to grow a group, increase its membership. As the membership increases, so will the average attendance. It's simply a fact of life and the way the "groups universe" works. Second, because 50% of group members are not present each time the group comes together, group leaders have a lot of work to do to reach out to the absentees in between meetings. That's a pretty good argument for keeping groups smaller—and not having large "pastor's classes" that have fifty or more people in attendance. I prefer to have groups with a maximum attendance of twenty. This means there are approximately forty people on the group's ministry list, and that requires lots of follow-up with absentees each week.

82

Eighty two percent. Keep that number in mind for just a moment.

Group leaders may not hear the words "Thank you" enough. They are some of the most important people in our churches. We may not express thanks often enough for the hours that group leaders spend studying, praying, and serving the members and guests who attend their groups.

Well, I'd like to say, "Thank you" if you are a group leader. You are making a real difference in people's lives. You're closing your church's "back door." What you do is so very important to the health of your church. It means a lot to the people in your group. How do I know this? Just take a look at what the research says. Numbers don't lie.

Dr. Thom Rainer discovered some important and disturbing information through research for his book, *High Expectations*. As he examined the attendance patterns of two groups of people—those who attended worship only and those who attended both worship and a Bible study group, he learned that of the people who attended both worship and Sunday School, 82% were still active after five years from joining a church. Of those who attended only worship, just 16% remained active.[57]

Take a church with 150 people in worship. For the sake of argument, let's say that fifty people attend worship only, and 100 people attend both Sunday School and worship. Based on Dr. Rainer's research, five years from now eighty two of the 100 people in Sunday School will still be around. But of those who attend worship only, a dismal eight of those fifty will still be connected to the church—just eight.

Do groups and group leaders matter to the church? You'd better believe it. If you are a group leader, you are helping people "stick" to the church. If you teach an adult group, you help those adults connect to people in your group, and you also help entire families stay connected to the church because those adults in your group most likely have kids in other parts of the ministry. If the adults stay connected, entire families stay connected.

4

I am amazed at how few churches actually have a plan for training group leaders. The lack of training may be because a staff leader and/or the church doesn't have a history of providing this. And it might be that the budget has never been adjusted upward to make ongoing training possible.

I've heard some staff leaders lament, "Even if we had ongoing training, no one would come." I don't believe that for a second. People do want to be trained. People want to do a good job at the things we've asked of them.

Why do we believe we don't need to be trained, when every other industry around us knows differently? How much longer will we let this trend go on? For the sake of the church, I hope not much longer.

Remember that the Georgia Baptist Convention surveyed approximately 2,500 churches in their state, asking the question, "How frequently do you train your group leaders?" Then the growth of those churches was tabulated over a four-year period, and the results were examined. The big takeaway? Churches that provided ongoing training at least four times a year grew at a rate of between 13 and 14%. Could there have been other factors like pastoral leadership in the pulpit? Probably. But the one factor we can put our finger on is the frequency at which training was conducted. Churches with less frequent training grew at a much smaller rate (4.2%), and those churches that chose not to train at all declined by 2.1%. Training matters. The number four reminds us that quarterly training can be a good starting point for creating a culture that values and benefits from regular training.

FOR FURTHER THOUGHT

1. Which of these metrics most excites you? Causes you to be concerned? Why?

2. If you had time and resources to focus on two of these, which two do you need to improve the most at your church?

3. How could you honor group leaders who are key to helping people connect relationally in your church?

4. Because people are taking longer to join the church today, how can you encourage group leaders to actively pursue guests over the long haul? What kinds of checks and balances will you incorporate to make sure that follow-up is being done?

ESSENTIAL 10: FOLLOW UP FANATICALLY

My family and I spent the better part of a year searching for a new church home after moving to the Nashville area. I was dismayed by the lack of follow-up when we visited churches. Only two churches contacted us to thank us for visiting; no group leaders did. We filled out visitor cards in every worship service and class we attended, but follow-up with our family was almost non-existent. We felt discouraged, unwanted, and unimportant. If we had not had such a strong church background, we might have given up the search. It was disheartening in the extreme.

If you want to have a healthier Sunday School, people must believe you want them there. Group leaders, group members, and church staff must follow up fanatically or else the church will inadvertently send a message that communicates, "You're not that important to us." That's a terrible message.

We recently traded in my wife's car for a new one (used, actually, but new to her). Later that day, our salesman called and left a voicemail, thanking us for patronizing his dealership and buying a car from him. He called a day later to make sure we were happy with the purchase, and to see if we had any questions about the car. His follow-up was excellent. He followed up fanatically. It's a sad commentary when the world does a better job of follow-up than the church does.

Over the years I've identified some principles of follow-up that are in effect no matter where your church is located. Here is a brief summary of those key principles of follow-up. See if these ring true from your experience.

PRINCIPLE #1: YOU CAN BE TOO AGGRESSIVE IN YOUR FOLLOW-UP.
Guests are on a "blind date" with your church. They don't know what to expect and are often very anxious. (If you've ever been on a blind date, you

know what I'm talking about.) Let's pretend for a moment that you are walking up to the doorstep of a young lady's house. The two of you have agreed to go on a blind date. She opens the door, and you are instantly taken aback by her charm and beauty. You drop to one knee and produce an engagement ring in a velvet-lined box you had hidden in your right pocket. You present it to her on the doorstep of her house and exclaim, "Will you marry me?" What is her answer going to be? Don't ask guests to "marry" your church too fast. That will ruin the "courtship." Instead, be ready to "date" that guest and to court them.

It's perfectly fine for a guest to be invited to have his or her name placed on a Bible study group's ministry role so the guest receives updates from the group and invitations to fellowships, ministry projects, and special events. This is very different than asking a person to join your church. Joining a group is not the same thing as joining the church. In fact, it's a good idea for guests to become members of groups before they even join the church.

PRINCIPLE #2: CONTACT BY GROUP MEMBERS IS MORE EFFECTIVE THAN CONTACT BY CHURCH STAFF.

If you want to make a positive impression on a guest, group members must reach out before a representative from the church staff does. Guests know that a call or email from a member of the staff is most likely part of the church's weekly outreach efforts. Staff are paid to do these kinds of things, but when a lay person takes the time to say, "Thanks for visiting our group," it means something different. This kind of follow-up impresses guests and breathes life into Sunday School.

A friend of mine, Wayne Poling, compiled a book on essential Sunday School work. He addressed the importance of follow-up and the importance of involving group members. He said, "Developing a strategy for contacting a first-time guest is critical to your church's future…Because the pastor and staff will most likely make some type of contact with each guest, a major key to your outreach organization will be to create a system where you can assist members in taking the next steps…Because your church members live in various subdivisions and local communities around your church, utilize their geographic proximity to the prospects who visit your church.

Enlist individuals from various geographic locations around your church who would be willing to make a simple follow-up contact with people from their neighborhood."[58] My friend's point is that you must have a strategy. Encourage group members to follow up with guests, and perhaps assign prospects to group members based on where they live, as he suggests. The bottom line is, have a plan. Implement a strategy. Some plan is better than no plan.

A survey indicates that the impact of a home visit is reduced by approximately 50% when made by a church staff member rather than people from a Sunday School class.[59] Guests will assume that contact from staff is a part of their job description, but they really appreciate a call, email, or home visit by one of their peers who is excited about the church. By now you get the picture: follow-up is important, and follow-up by group members is best. How will you encourage your groups to connect with their guests?

PRINCIPLE #3: THE SOONER YOU MAKE CONTACT, THE BETTER.

A survey has demonstrated that if guests are contacted within thirty-six hours, first-time guests return 85% of the time. If contacted within seventy-two hours, first-time guests return 60% of the time. If contacted seven days after the initial visit, only 15% of first-time guests return the next week.[60]

Making a home visit may seem like a lot of trouble, a time-waster, and something from a bygone era, but it can still be an effective way to reach people for Sunday School and church membership. I don't recommend unannounced visits, but I have found that setting appointments is an effective way to make sure someone is home. I also don't recommend long visits. Even a "porch" visit that is made quickly can communicate the church's desire to have the guest return for a second visit.

PRINCIPLE #4: FOLLOW-UP IS A MARATHON, NOT A SPRINT.

According to research, people are taking up to eighteen months to join a church today. It's very important that group leaders be consistent in the way they lead their members to follow up with guests. An initial call or email is great, but because people are taking so long to join, a group must approach follow-up more like a marathon than a sprint. Regular contact and invitations to return to the group are needed to keep people connected to your group.

Patience and follow-up are the keys to moving people from being attenders to becoming members. Plan on a long courtship, and don't give up!

PRINCIPLE #5: IF GUESTS VISIT THREE CONSECUTIVE SUNDAYS, YOU'LL LIKELY RETAIN THEM.

An outreach firm that specializes in helping churches assimilate people reported some exciting statistics at one of their annual training events. As I participated in one of the workshops, I learned that:

- 10% of all first-time guests will become members.
- 25% of all second-time guests will become members.
- 45% of all third-time guests will become members.[61]

You get the idea. A guest who returns to your church on consecutive Sundays begins to develop a routine, relationships, and a familiarity with your church's schedule, layout, and ministries. It makes it more difficult to leave and go to another place where they have to start all over from scratch. In essence, when a person attends multiple weeks in a row, you've made the pain of switching much greater.

PRINCIPLE #6: ONE SIZE DOES NOT FIT ALL WHEN IT COMES TO FOLLOWING UP WITH GUESTS

Because of people's busy lifestyles, expectations of churches, and generational preferences, your church needs multiple "hooks in the water," to borrow a fishing term. Some people will prefer that you visit them in their homes. Others will be just as pleased with a phone call, email, or a letter from the pastor. Still others won't mind a text message, a Facebook message, or even a short meeting for coffee or lunch.

10 THINGS GUESTS WISHED WE KNEW

It's tough being the outsider looking to connect to a new church and a new Bible study group. It's not easy. In fact, if you've been a member of a church and/or a Bible study group for a few years, you've most likely forgotten how hard it is to find a church home and a Bible study group to belong to. Let's try and put ourselves into the position of our guests. If we asked guests about their experiences at church and our attempts to assimilate them into our groups, here are some things they'd want us to know:

1. **We are anxious.** Visiting a new church can be a scary experience. It's hard to know how to dress (Do I dress up or down?), where to park, and which door to enter. Chances are I won't know your songs of worship, nor will I be as familiar with the Bible as you are. And it seems like everyone in your Bible study group is a Bible expert compared to me.

2. **We evaluate everything.** The moment we come onto your church campus, we are in "evaluation mode." Nothing escapes our scrutiny, because little things tell us a lot about you and your congregation. Was there a directional sign pointing me to guest parking? Did a parking lot greeter help me out of the car and into the right building? Was the bathroom clean? Are the preschool classrooms equipped with proper toys and learning aids? Were there enough volunteers? Did things seem chaotic or did the church's lay leaders know what they were doing? Was there dust on the leaves of that ficus tree in the corner?

3. **We feel like outsiders.** As friendly as you try to be to me, I'm still the outsider. You have your friendships; it's apparent because you talk with your friends much more than you talk to me. I wish I knew your inside jokes; I'd laugh along, too (but for now I'll just have to listen in). It's been three minutes since I've sat down in the classroom, and so far, no one's introduced themselves. Because of the looks people are giving me, did I just sit in their pew? You're studying what? I don't have one of those books that your group members have. I dressed up again, and it looks like you're a pretty casual church. Great.

4. **We are hopeful.** The reason I'm visiting your church is because I want to connect with you. I need friends. I want a place where I can belong. I even believe I have some gifts and abilities that God might want to use at your church. I hope there's a place for me to serve. I really want to like your pastor, your people, and your programs.

5. **We don't want to be identified until we're ready.** The one thing you will do to make me feel really uncomfortable is to make me identify myself before I'm ready. Don't ask me to stand while the congregation

remains seated, and don't ask the congregation to stand while I remain seated. That's awkward for all of us. I want to let you know who I am at my own pace. I'll fill out your visitor information card when I'm ready. It may take me weeks of visiting your church before I'm ready to give you any of my personal contact information.

6. **We are influenced by our kids' experiences at church.** Your church service and the Bible study we attended were really good. In fact, it was a good day. At this point we're really hopeful that this might be the place we land. But before we can make a decision about all that, I need to know how you treated my kids. So, the first question I'm going to ask my children is, "Did you like it?" I'm not going to start with "What did you learn in Sunday School?" or some other more appropriate question. If my kids had a bad experience, I'm not going to force them to come back. If my kids had a great experience, though, and I didn't, I'm highly likely to tolerate that since my kids are happy.

7. **We are not in a hurry to join your church.** We are not going to be rushed. In fact, we aren't really "joiners" in the first place. We're going to attend your church because the preaching is good. We're going to go to small groups at the church down the street because they learned our names and were very welcoming. There's even another church that has great worship, and we love the concerts they occasionally do for the members and the community. We're in no rush. We're just going to take our time and see what happens. If you want to keep me interested in your church, you're going to have to do continual follow-up for a long time.

8. **Our first impression of the church is hard to overcome if it's negative.** The first seven minutes we are on your church campus are really critical in helping us decide if this is the right place or not. You've heard the expression, "You never get a second chance to make a first impression." It may be overused, but it's true.

9. **Our last impression of the church is hard to overcome if it's negative.** I don't want to put any pressure on you, but even if we've had a really good experience at your church, it can be ruined by the

last thing that happens to us. I know that's not fair, but it's just the way it is. If you ignore me after the church service or head off to lunch without smiling or being neighborly, you remind me that I'm not part of your club. You can do everything just right and still trip up at the finish line. You've got to pay attention to what I'm experiencing all morning long.

10. **The church doesn't get bonus points for being friendly.** Guess what? I'm glad that you think you have a friendly church. But you don't get any extra points for that because you are a church! You're supposed to be friendly! Dr. Thom Rainer discovered that, "Most church members do not view themselves as unfriendly. But they do not see themselves from the perspective of church guests. They don't usually speak to guests because they don't know them. And the church members usually retreat to the comfort of the holy huddles of the people they do know."[62]

6 WAYS THAT BIBLE STUDY GROUPS CAN HELP CONNECT PEOPLE DURING AND AFTER THEIR VISIT

If a Bible study group is functioning as an open group, then it's designed to reach new people. In fact, the group leader and the group's members are most likely on the lookout for new people. If you want to make your guests feel welcome when they drop by, do the following:

1. **Wear name tags.** My friend David Francis believes in this, and I do too. I've seen how important inexpensive stick-on name tags are when guests attended my group's study. The Bible study group I once led expected to have guests. Giving group members a name tag to fill out and wear was part of my group's strategy for assimilating guests into our group. "Name tags can be a reminder of mission and a symbol of faith. Seriously? Absolutely! They say, 'We are expecting God to send someone new to the group this week.'…Some people do and will make fun of me for the nametag stuff. I don't care. It's a stickable strategy. Stick with it for six months."[63]

2. **Sit in a circle.** If your room is arranged in rows of chairs, consider sitting in a large circle. People are more likely to speak up and

participate if they can see each other's faces. Circles and half-circles create conversational community.

3. **Introduce guests to group members.** Take the initiative and introduce guests to people in your group. Some folks are pretty shy, and they need a little push to start talking to one another. Even better: have a designated greeter or greeters in your group whose job it is to reach out to your guests and introduce them to others.

4. **Make sure your meeting place has extra chairs.** There's nothing more "neighborly" than having plenty of seating for guests, and if your meeting place is arranged in rows, please don't make guests sit "up front."

5. **Call guests by name during the Bible study.** Wearing name tags will help you do this! Don't put a guest on the spot, but do affirm any answer they provide. "John, that's a great insight. Thank you for sharing that with our group."

6. **Invite the guest back.** Don't let a guest leave your Bible study group without asking them to please join you again the next time your group meets. Don't just assume they'll come back.

FOR FURTHER THOUGHT

1. How would you evaluate your overall response time when reaching out to guests? Do you typically contact guests within the first few hours, days, or weeks of their initial visit?

2. What barriers are keeping you from doing a better job of following up with your guests more quickly?

3. What can you do to encourage guests to attend your church and a Bible study group several weeks in a row?

4. Which of the ten things guests wished we knew can you address through your church's website? Bible study groups? Where is the low-hanging fruit?

11

ESSENTIAL 11: PROVIDE ONGOING STUDIES

I was recently asked a great question by a pastor. He wanted to know what he should say when group leaders in his church asked the question, "Do we have to use curriculum? Why can't we just teach the Bible?" To quote one of my favorite Sunday School champions, Arthur Flake, "Whenever the Bible is adequately or intelligently studied, there must be a definite, comprehensive plan—a guide for the work...The Bible is a gigantic storehouse of all kinds of riches...This great truth is the very reason why there must be a plan for its study...Such is the place of lesson literature...The literature carries a well-conceived, definite, comprehensive, and continuous plan for the study of the Bible."[64]

This fellow went on to share a tremendous illustration that I'll never forget. Imagine a group of friends following a guide through an underground cavern, their skillful guide enthusiastically explaining relevant information about the underground formations. Ropes, flashlights, and a spirit of adventure and daring made for an exciting and memorable exploration. While the group of friends might have negotiated the trip without a guide, much of the wonder would have been lost or misunderstood, or even gone unappreciated. So it is with the Sunday School curriculum your church chooses to use. In the hands of a teacher, it serves to guide people in their exploration of the Scriptures, depending upon the Holy Spirit to illuminate and guide the entire study. The curriculum is a means to an end, not the end itself. The Bible will always be the chief curriculum in the Sunday School.

The bottom line is that your Sunday School will be healthier when you use an ongoing curriculum strategy. If you want to breathe life into your Sunday School, make sure that your groups are using ongoing curriculum.

WHY USE CURRICULUM?

I've dealt with similar questions to the one above in the course of serving three churches. The question about curriculum is a fair and valid one. I would answer the question, "Why should we use curriculum?" like this:

1. **Because ongoing Bible studies lead people to study the Bible.** Ongoing studies do not replace the Bible. In fact, they do just the opposite. Authors and writers use their expertise and backgrounds to help group members understand and apply the Bible to life. The ongoing study materials increase attention on the sacred Scriptures. The Bible remains the centerpiece of every study. Ongoing materials positively enhance the study of God's Word.

2. **Because we want to get people into the Word daily.** Discipleship doesn't take a week off, but group members do. Isn't it a good idea to place something like a PSG (Personal Study Guide) in their hands so they have content to study between group sessions? This allows them to keep up with the group, even when they are not present. Disciples should read God's Word daily, and Personal Study Guides help them do just that. Dr. Brad Waggoner discovered through his research that the number one predictor of year-over-year spiritual growth was whether or not a believer reads God's Word daily.[65]

3. **Because the content is trustworthy.** Teachers in your church and mine have all kinds of theological backgrounds. Some group leaders may have been in church for a long time. Others may be much newer to your church and denomination. Because church leaders are commanded to guard doctrine closely, it matters what teachers teach. Turning them loose to teach anything they want opens the door to doctrine being introduced into your church that is contrary to your church's beliefs. When you provide an ongoing curriculum for your groups, teachers are held more accountable because both they and their group members have curriculum from which they are studying. Heresy has almost no chance of surviving when an ongoing curriculum is used. Someone in the group will recognize the error and hold the group leader accountable.

4. **Because the Bible studies are crafted by teams of experts.** If your child just turned sixteen and was going to drive to the mall for the first time alone, would you feel better about letting her drive a car designed by one engineer or a team of engineers? You know as well as I do you'd say, "A team of engineers." That's because there are experts in braking systems, electrical systems, power steering, and much more. A car designed by a team is a much better car. It works the same way when it comes to Bible study materials. Would you prefer that group members are led by one person who has created a Bible study, or led by a person whose Bible study materials were intentionally crafted by a team of curriculum experts? I sat in a group in which a well-meaning teacher had crafted his own Bible study from scratch. On that day we studied the story of Joseph and Mary, and the birth of Christ. The group leader asked us a question he'd created, "Why did Joseph make a mistake in choosing to divorce Mary?" I thought about that for a moment, raised my hand, and said, "Excuse me, but Joseph did not make a mistake. He was within his legal rights. He had been described as a righteous man earlier in the passage. He put Mary away quietly because he loved her and did not want to bring shame to her. And as soon as the angel told him to take Mary to be his wife, he did." The teacher was perplexed. People in the group said, "Hey, that's right!" This is what can happen when just one person crafts a Bible study. No one reads it for content, clarity, and accuracy before it is taught.

5. **Because curriculum is an affordable investment in spiritual growth.** It may be surprising to know that you could equip a group leader with a leader guide, a commentary, a leader pack (with posters and other visual aids), and ten Personal Study Guides for the group members all for about $65 every ninety days! If you divide that by the thirteen weeks in the quarter, that's just $5 a week to equip a group of ten people to study the Bible. To take it to the extreme, it's $.72 per day, which is less than a pack of breath mints.

6. **Because we want guests to feel equipped.** By providing curriculum for guests, the church helps them fit into existing groups. Some guests will not have strong church backgrounds. Attending a Bible study is a big step for them. In fact, some guests feel very intimidated to come into groups where everyone appears to have a firm grasp of the Bible. A Personal Study Guide helps guests read ahead and be prepared for class discussion about the Bible. "It's a good and right thing to expect members to come prepared for the class session. That's one advantage of providing inexpensive printed curriculum materials...Along with your invitation [for guests to come back] you can provide a copy of the study material you are using. If you are using 'ongoing' material... you can say something like, 'Here's a booklet with the topics and Scriptures we're studying in our class right now. Before you come, you might want to take a few minutes to find the study for that weekend in the book and read ahead'...By that simple act, you've removed the number one barrier for adults: thinking they know too little about the Bible to participate."[66]

7. **Because group members need balanced Bible study.** Curriculum is designed on a "scope and sequence," which is the sum of all the topics that will be covered and the order in which they are studied. Curriculum publishers work hard to make sure that people receive "the whole counsel of God" over time. When group leaders prepare their own studies, they often gravitate to familiar topics and doctrines that are important to them, creating imbalanced approaches to studying the Bible. Curriculum ensures that growing disciples receive a balanced diet from God's Word over time.

8. **Because every church needs new group leaders.** Not every person you recruit to become a group leader will be able to prepare Bible studies on his or her own. If ongoing curriculum is provided, there will be leader helps to guide the group leader in what to say and do. Ongoing curriculum gives group leaders confidence, and it saves them many hours of searching for the next Bible study.

Some Bible study groups do not utilize Personal Study Guides. I know from experience that curriculum enhances the group Bible study time. When I was a group leader, I incorporated the PSG (Personal Study Guide) into my group's Bible study time by continually doing all of the following:

1. Ask a group member to be prepared to share a summary of a section of the PSG.

2. Email/Message/Facebook group members and ask for their response to a particular quote on a page in the PSG.

3. During Bible study, break the group into smaller groups to compare responses to an assigned part of the study.

4. Encourage the use of the application questions in small groups during the group study.

5. Record prayer requests in the Personal Study Guide.

6. Refer to study questions throughout the group Bible study.

7. Ask a group member to present a brief report on a doctrine, person, or event that is in the Personal Study Guide.

8. Remind the group members of their responsibility in the discipling process, and the PSG's part in that.

9. Have group members create accountability partners who use content from the PSG to encourage spiritual growth.

OVERCOMING THE "IT'S NOT DEEP ENOUGH" OBJECTION

One of the most frustrating things said by well-meaning Bible study group members (or group leaders) is, "Sunday School isn't deep enough." Maybe someone has said that to you as a group leader. Perhaps you're a pastor or you lead your church's education ministry and group members have said the same thing to you. What can you say to help them understand more fully the Sunday School's mission, the curriculum chosen by the church, and the depth of content? Plenty.

1. **Sunday School isn't designed to be deep.** People who have been in Sunday School groups for a long time may have forgotten that Sunday School is supposed to be an evangelistic outreach ministry. It is designed to be attractional and to provide a place for every member and guest to easily find a place where they belong. Too many groups have turned their focus inward, and that leads to the complaint that lessons aren't deep enough. Our groups are filled with members who

should have been encouraged to leave their groups to start other ones, or to take leadership roles in another ministry of the church, but they sit in groups year after year. They hear Bible studies over and over on familiar topics and texts, and it's no wonder they complain about a lack of depth—they know the Bible stories backwards and forwards, and they should be leading groups of their own! If Sunday School is truly going to be an open group ministry (open to new people attending each week), then we must assume that some of those people won't have a great grasp of the Bible, and they'll need foundational discipleship lessons as they grow up in Christ. Open groups have Bible studies that are accessible to "Joe Unconnected" who comes to the group with little or no Bible background. If groups had "deep" Bible study each week, it would potentially discourage people like Joe Unconnected who needs a Bible study he can understand and apply.

2. **Sunday School can be used to create D-Groups.** To make sure that Sunday School remains open to new people attending weekly, it is imperative that the curriculum chosen is designed on a solid open-group philosophy. That means lessons stand alone and create a satisfying Bible study experience for each group member. It means that lessons are crafted with the assumption that people of all spiritual maturity levels will be present. But to answer the need of some more mature group members for more depth of study, Sunday School group leaders should seriously consider starting D-Groups through their class. What's a D-Group, you ask? D-Groups are same-sex groups of three to four people who meet during the week for more in-depth study and accountability. By sponsoring D-Groups, Sunday School classes can remain open to prospective new members being in attendance, deliver satisfying Bible study lessons, but save the "depth" for another time when those group members who really desire it can meet together.

3. **No one can truly define what they mean by "depth."** If you ask two people what they mean by "deeper Bible study" or "depth," you'll get three answers! For some people depth means studying a lot of verses or every verse in a passage. For others, depth means that Greek or

Hebrew backgrounds of words are regularly explored and sometimes the tense, mood, and voice of those words. For still other people, depth means learning a new factoid they've never heard before.

4. **We are all educated beyond our level of obedience.** It makes no sense to ask for depth when we aren't obeying what we already know to be the revealed will of God. There is actually depth in simplicity. Bible studies that help people focus on simple truths from God's Word they should be living out, but are not, can challenge them to live out the Word in front of family, friends, neighbors, and peers. What people don't need is another fact about a Bible character. What they don't need is another list of things that happened on a particular plot of ground in the Bible. What we *do* need is to love our neighbors and to love God with all our heart, mind, soul, and strength. What we need is to be the Christian spouse, employee, and friend they need us to be. Teach me something simple and give me practical ways to live it out. There's depth! I don't need another history lesson. I need a road map for living life in a way that pleases God.

FOR FURTHER THOUGHT

1. What are the most important benefits of using ongoing curriculum? How does this (or would this) be advantageous for your church?

2. How confident are you that the group leaders in your church are teaching in agreement with your church's statement of faith?

3. Of the various reasons for using curriculum in the "Why Use Curriculum?" section of the chapter, which two reasons are most compelling in your current ministry context?

4. Does your church have a clear, consistent plan for teaching the Bible in all age groups? How would you articulate that plan to a guest who has asked, "So, what will our family study if we attend your Bible study groups?"

12

ESSENTIAL 12: ADOPT A PHILOSOPHY

Pastors, Christian educators, and other church leaders should be eager to develop a philosophy of education. A philosophy of education informs the choices we make, and those choices ultimately affect the lives of people. A leader's philosophy about Christian education has far-reaching implications for members of the local church.

A statement of philosophy, therefore, is foundational to anyone who guides the Sunday School and discipleship ministries in the church, whether the person is formally educated or a lay volunteer leader. Because of the transformative and eternal implications of the work of Christian education, developing a formal statement of educational philosophy is important, because it serves as a guide to the Christian educator as he goes about fulfilling his ministry calling.

The lack of formalizing one's philosophy of ministry leads to erratic and inconsistent decisions about curriculum, class size, purpose, and much more. It's one reason that many churches' Sunday Schools are not healthy; poor choices have been made over the years.

It's imperative that the people charged with the responsibility of growing and developing a church's Bible teaching ministry have a clear understanding about their philosophy of education.

A PHILOSOPHY OF CHRISTIAN EDUCATION

After years of serving the church as an education/discipleship pastor, and after serving as a group leader for a number of years, I have clarified my definition of Christian education, aligning it with biblical principles and real-world experience.

The statement that follows guides me as I lead my church to make numerous decisions about our Sunday School and discipleship strategies. Don't feel like you have to copy and paste this statement and use it at your church. Use this as a guide. Let it inform a statement that you develop for yourself and your ministry context.

My philosophy of Christian education is: "the intentional focusing on the Bible by a group of people seeking to become spiritually mature. This group may include believers and non-believers who are guided by a prepared, obedient, Holy Spirit-empowered leader who uses a variety of methods to minister to them and redemptively engage them in the learning process, resulting in the spiritual transformation of the group members as evidenced by their growing obedience to Jesus' commands."

The rationale and biblical support for this philosophy statement is below. The statement has been divided into smaller sections in order to deal with the implications and meanings of various parts of my definition of Christian education.

CHRISTIAN EDUCATION IS THE INTENTIONAL FOCUSING ON THE BIBLE

The Bible is the focus of all Christian education. It is simple enough for a child to comprehend ("and you know that from infancy you have known the sacred Scriptures, which are able to give you wisdom for salvation through faith in Christ Jesus…" 2 Tim. 3:15), yet complex enough that it can take a lifetime to master. "All Scripture is inspired by God and is useful for teaching, training, rebuking, and correcting" (2 Tim. 3:16-17). The Bible must be the place where the focus of the learner is placed.

Southern Baptists have long been identified as a "people of the Word." There could be no greater moniker. The Bible is God's Word and His revelation to mankind. Southern Baptists have affirmed the centrality of the Scriptures and their importance to the church and to individual believers. Contained within the *Baptist Faith and Message's* statement about the Bible are multiple reasons why it must be the central focus of Christian education:

"The Holy Bible was written by men divinely inspired and is God's revelation of Himself to man. It is a perfect treasure of divine instruction. It has God for its author, salvation for its end, and truth, without any mixture of error, for its matter. Therefore, all Scripture is totally true and trustworthy. It reveals the principles by which God judges us, and therefore is, and will remain to the end of the world, the true center of Christian union, and the supreme standard by which all human conduct, creeds, and religious opinions should be tried. All Scripture is a testimony to Christ, who is Himself the focus of divine revelation."[67]

The Scriptures, therefore, are the focus of Christian education because they point people to Christ, who, as the Baptist Faith and Message states, is the focus of God's divine revelation to mankind. Without the divine revelation, we would have nothing on which to focus our Christian education efforts. We would be a people without content, but more importantly, we would be a people without hope.

BY A GROUP OF PEOPLE

Christian education takes place within the context of a group of people. The Book of Genesis begins with a community of people, Adam, Eve, and God, in relationship with one another. Ed Stetzer and Eric Geiger explain, "A theology of community begins here because we were created for community. So, when we recreate biblical community, we are returning people to the environment for which God created us."[68] Jesus' ministry was primarily to a group of twelve men and a smaller inner circle of three disciples. The calling of the first disciples provides an example of group life and how a diverse group of people can come together, experience community, failure, and success, and the transformative nature of God's Word on individuals. It was in small groups that the early church gathered (Acts 2:46), and the practice of organizing people into groups continues today.

Groups gather together to study the Bible, receive encouragement, provide support, and participate in prayer. Group members' lives intersect as they grow spiritually, sharing stories of God's redemptive work in their lives. Through group Bible studies, people engage in ministry to others in the group. At times the group ministers to people who are outside the Christian faith.

It's in the context of groups that leaders explain and interpret Scripture, guiding people to understand and obey it. Such was the case in Nehemiah 8.

The Word of God was read by Ezra to the people, and a group of Levites "explained the law to the people as they stood in their places. They read out of the book of the law of God, translating and giving the meaning so the people would understand what was read" (Neh. 8:7-8). The Levites, strategically positioned throughout the crowd of people, taught and explained the law of God to smaller groups of people. The people needed others who were skilled and trained to help them understand and apply what they had heard. Without these groups, the people would have been at a disadvantage to fully understand and act upon God's Word.

LifeWay's research on discipleship has been published in the book *Transformational Groups*. The research demonstrated the spiritual benefits of being involved in a group Bible study. The research proved that people who are in a group serve more than those who are not in a group. The research also proved that people in groups share more of their finances and serve at a higher percentage than do people who are not committed to a group. There are other benefits, too. People in groups share their faith more frequently than those who are not in a group, and people in groups pray more than those who are not in a group.[69] Discipleship best takes place within the context of groups.

SEEKING TO BECOME SPIRITUALLY MATURE

A goal of Christian education is the spiritual transformation of believers. The Lord's desire is to mature His disciples into more fully devoted followers. Hebrews 6:1 says, "Therefore, let us leave the elementary teaching about Christ and go on to maturity, not laying again a foundation of repentance from dead works…" The apostle Peter wrote about the need for believers to grow and mature in their faith when he wrote the words, "Like newborn infants, desire the pure milk of the word, so that you may grow up into your salvation…" (1 Pet. 2:2).

The spiritual growth of believers takes place both corporately and privately. Christian educator and author Robert Pazmino states, "Christian education efforts must seriously evaluate the extent to which persons are encouraged to grow in their personal relationship with God—provided a concern for the private sphere does not neglect the public and corporate responsibilities of Christians."[70] Personal and corporate maturation opportunities work in tandem. We grow together spiritually in groups, but we also grow spiritually in our personal and private time with the Lord as we read, study, and meditate on His Word.

THIS GROUP MAY INCLUDE BELIEVERS AND NON-BELIEVERS

Should a group of people who are intentionally studying the Bible with a goal of spiritual maturity also include non-believers? The answer is yes. Teachers play a part in God's redemptive work in the world. In *A Theology for Christian Education,* author James R. Estep, Jr. explains, "Education must have transformation as its redemptive and salvific element if it is to be Christian. The evangelistic work of the church cannot be separated from the educational ministry of the church since both conversion and nurture through instruction are essential for the transformation of individuals into Christlike disciples...God as our Redeemer reminds Christian educators that evangelism is not a separate task from education, both must coalesce to fulfill the mission of the church."[71]

Open groups have been part of the church landscape for many decades. Sunday School, perhaps the best-known open-group Bible study strategy, anticipates that outsiders might be present in Bible study. It is in this context that non-believers are able to study with maturing Christians. Non-believers are exposed to the Bible, challenged to surrender their lives to Christ, and given opportunities to observe the lives of their fellow group members who are Christ-followers. It is in this kind of setting that non-believers are exposed to the gospel, to Christians, and to opportunities to receive Christ as Savior. These non-believers, who are spiritually far from God, may well become Christians as they experience group life, develop relationships with believers, and realize the genuineness of people's faith in Jesus Christ.

The involvement of non-believers in a Bible study group is foundational to the church's mission to "go and make disciples" (Matt. 28:18-20). Paul wrote to the church at Corinth and anticipated that non-believers would be part of the church's gathering. He wrote, "If, therefore, the whole church assembles together....and people who are outsiders or unbelievers come in..." (1 Cor. 14:23). It's to God's glory that groups are open to outsiders for the purpose of leading them to repentance and faith.

GUIDED BY A PREPARED,
OBEDIENT, HOLY SPIRIT-EMPOWERED LEADER

The word "guided" is a term that suggests several important ideas. Guiding a group of people to study the Bible requires patience, skill, and care. Guiding implies relationship, whereas "instructing" or "teaching" would suggest a more formal environment in which the goal was to transfer information from the leader to the learner. When a teacher engages in relationship with his learners, he takes risks. Robert Pazmino explains that this "places the teacher in a position of risk and vulnerability in loving and interacting with students. This interaction requires the sharing of one's very life and the willingness to serve as an example in guiding others."[72] When teachers serve as guides, they do so with the intent to participate in the group not only as its guide, but also as a fellow learner and sojourner. The apostle Paul implored the Corinthian believers to "Imitate me, as I also imitate Christ" (1 Cor. 11:1). Paul's obedience was something to be seen and imitated by other believers. This prepared, obedient, Holy Spirit-empowered leader provided a lifestyle that was to be an example to the Christians at Corinth.

Group leaders must be prepared, and they must be obedient to the Bible's teachings as maturing disciples in order to be effective leaders. Ezra 7:10 says, "Now Ezra had determined in his heart to study the law of the LORD, obey it, and teach its statutes and ordinances in Israel" (Ezra 7:10). Ezra determined that he should first study the law of the Lord, and then obey it. Only after he had done these two things did he attempt to teach the Word of God to the people of Israel. This is the correct order for leaders of Bible study groups. Ezra's preparation included diligent, repeated study. The original Hebrew communicates an important word picture. In the original language, "study" literally meant "to tread frequently over, as in pursuit." This should be the goal of every Christian teacher. He or she must go over and over God's Word as they pursue its meaning; Christian teachers are "on the hunt" for God's truth. Once that truth is captured in their minds and hearts, it is obeyed. As obedient, authentic followers of God, teachers are then able to stand before God's people and challenge them to obey it as well.

Christian educators are completely dependent upon the Holy Spirit for His empowerment and leadership in the learning process. "I am the vine; you are the branches. The one who remains in me and I in him produces much fruit, because you can do nothing without me" (John 15:5). Any group leader who attempts to lead without this empowerment will soon find himself serving in his own strength, not God's strength. In *A Theology for Christian Education*, Michael J. Anthony explains, "As teachers we need to be reminded of our dependency on the Holy Spirit to speak to students in their hearts where lasting life transformation takes place…changing habits of the heart requires heart surgery, not brain surgery, and that is what the Holy Spirit brings to the learning encounter."[73]

WHO USES A VARIETY OF METHODS

Predictable. That word describes the Bible study experience in too many groups. Leaders often teach in the same way they prefer to learn, and they almost never deviate from favored methods. According to Anthony, it's important that as Christian educators, "We use a variety of methods in our instruction today because, like seasoning in a meal, we prefer variety. It brings out what's special and allows particular elements of the lesson to stand out beyond others. As teachers, our weakest method is the one we use the most. That's why we need variety but not just for variety's sake."[74] Teaching that lacks variety will lead to boredom in Bible study, and that kind of Bible study will not be effective. Teaching that is predictable is exactly the opposite of the way in which God communicated in the Old and New Testaments.

In the Old Testament, God the Father communicated "at different times and in different ways" (Heb. 1:1). God communicated visually through the rainbow and the cloud of fire by night. He communicated in such a way that people's senses were engaged (the Egyptian plagues are a good example of this). His style of communication was captivating, like at the banquet in Daniel 5 when a hand appeared and wrote on the wall for all to see. God also communicated in unexpected ways, such as Balaam's talking donkey.

In the New Testament, Jesus taught using a variety of methods. At times He lectured. Sometimes He engaged people in debate and discussion. At times He communicated visually (He pointed to the temple and told His disciples that it would ultimately be destroyed; He called a little child from among them to teach about the kingdom of heaven).[75] Christian education requires teachers to use a variety of methods to communicate God's Word to group members. Variety emulates the way in which God the Father and His Son communicated throughout the Old and New Testaments.

TO MINISTER TO THEM

Teaching is an act of ministry and service to others. It allows teachers the opportunity to exercise their God-given spiritual gifts as they serve the body of Christ. Teachers minister to and serve both the mature and the maturing. A teacher who approaches the task of teaching with this mindset acts as a servant and lives out the "upside down" kingdom that Jesus described in Matthew 20. Jesus told His disciples, "Whoever wants to be great among you must be your servant, and whoever wants to be first among you must be your slave; just as the Son of Man did not come to be served, but to serve, and to give his life as a ransom for many" (Matt. 20:26-28). Serving and ministering to people is made possible as teachers guide their groups to know and live out the Bible. Teachers are ministers and shepherds to the flock of believers that God allows them to shepherd. As shepherd-leaders, they are ministers and co-laborers with Christ, setting aside their needs in order to more fully meet the needs of the people in their groups. Teaching is an act of service and ministry.

AND REDEMPTIVELY ENGAGE THEM

George Knight wrote, "Since the function of Christian education is one of reconciliation and restoring the balanced image of God in students, education should be seen primarily as a redemptive act. If education is viewed in that manner, then the role of the teacher is ministerial and pastoral in the sense that the teacher is an agent of reconciliation."[76] Christian education should engage the whole person. Each person has been created in the *imago Dei*, and as such deserves the teacher's respect and best efforts to help them in their quest to grow as disciples of Christ. The restoration of mankind is one of the great themes in the Bible, and as teachers engage with learners to apply God's Word, they participate with God in His redemptive efforts.

IN THE LEARNING PROCESS

The key word in this part of the definition is the word "process." People can be instructed in the Bible for a lifetime and still only scratch the surface of understanding, much less application. "Process" reminds us that groups will have people at all points on a discipleship continuum. Teachers must engage the more mature believers, while not leaving the less mature behind.

RESULTING IN THE SPIRITUAL TRANSFORMATION
OF THE GROUP MEMBERS

Information transfer has been the norm in many Bible study groups. Teachers have followed an education model that placed them at the center of the group session. In many groups, the teacher is one of only a few people who have prepared before the group Bible study experience. The goal in too many groups is for the well-prepared teacher to deliver a monologue with minimal engagement by members, resulting in a transfer of information.

Transformation, not information, is what is needed in Bible study groups. Anthony explains, "Our goal in Christian education is the spiritual maturity of our disciples: 'to present every man complete in Christ (Col. 1:28). The outcome of our lesson is usually not short-term behavior change… the outcome should be long-term life transformation."[77] The real goal of discipleship must be the spiritual transformation of Jesus' disciples, which is accompanied by an increasing appreciation and reverence for God. In his book, *Foundational Issues in Christian Education,* Robert Pazmino writes, "The Greeks learned in order to comprehend. The Hebrews learned in order to revere. The modern man learns in order to use. Whereas comprehension and the use of learning are important, the challenge remains for Christian educators to enable persons to revere, to appreciate, to stand in awe of and worship God as a result of their teaching."[78] A transformed life is one that increasingly understands, obeys, and stands amazed at God's grace to him.

AS EVIDENCED BY THEIR GROWING OBEDIENCE
TO JESUS' COMMANDS

The tell-tale sign of a growing disciple is his or her obedience to Jesus' commands (Matt. 28:18-20). There are numerous believers today who have been educated well beyond their level of obedience. This is one challenge facing Christianity today; it is a religion whose members are not viewed as authentic by outsiders. What is missing is obedience to the Bible's teachings. Even non-believers are able to spot a disingenuous Christian and reject Christianity based on behavior that does not rise to meet biblical standards. What the world needs to see are believers who know and obey Christ's commands daily. As long as believers do not increasingly obey the commands of Christ in Scripture, Christianity will struggle to differentiate itself from other religions. Outsiders want to know if Christianity "works." These "pre-Christians" might be persuaded to consider the claims of Christ if they observed believers who obeyed the sacred texts.

Group leaders today must create opportunities for the Holy Spirit to work in the lives of the group members. George R. Knight, in his book, *Philosophy & Education*, explains, "The task of education is to create learning environments that lead to desired behavior..."[79] The Christian teacher partners with the Holy Spirit to create opportunities to respond and submit to Christ's lordship. A culture of obedience to Christ's commands is created as individual believers understand and obey Jesus' instructions as revealed in the Old and New Testaments. Teaching that attempts to change behavior by only transferring information from teacher to learner will continue to fall short of making genuine disciples. Authentic disciples will love Jesus and obey His commands as a loving response to their Savior. As Samuel asked, "Does the LORD take pleasure in burnt offerings and sacrifices as much as in obeying the LORD? Look: to obey is better than sacrifice, to pay attention is better than the fat of rams" (1 Sam. 15:22). May our education efforts lead people to love God more and to love His Word to the point they obey it as they serve and follow Him.

FOR FURTHER THOUGHT

1. What is your philosophy of Christian education? How would you explain it to someone else?

2. Which parts of the philosophy statement presented in this chapter do you agree with? Disagree?

3. Why is having a clearly defined education philosophy so important to you? Your church?

4. Use the space below to jot down your primary takeaways from this chapter on adopting a philosophy.

13

IMPLEMENTING THE 12 ESSENTIALS

If you've made it this far, go just a little further. Press on and complete this chapter; it may be the most important one for breathing life into your Sunday School.

In order to help you process the content from the book so that it is really useful and meaningful to your church, complete the series of short assignments that follow. At the end of it all, you'll have a game plan for taking the first steps to breathe life into your Sunday School. But before we proceed, I want you to know the story of Bethlehem Steel. I first heard a friend, Wayne Poling, share this story with a large group of Sunday School leaders.

THE STORY OF BETHLEHEM STEEL

Many years ago, when Bethlehem Steel was a small up-and-coming factory, a young management consultant named Ivy Lee visited Charles Schwab, a manager of Bethlehem Steel. (Schwab later became the first man in history to earn a salary of a million dollars a year. Andrew Carnegie, founder of the company, liked Schwab's ability to accomplish things.)

Lee said that he could help Schwab find better ways to do the things necessary for the company's success. Schwab told him that they already knew how to make steel and knew what needed to be done. But, he added, they were not getting those things done. "Show me how to do the things we ought to be doing," Schwab challenged, "and we'll pay you whatever you want." Lee said that he could do that in twenty minutes. He even offered to let Schwab use the system and then pay Lee whatever the steel company executive thought it was worth, if anything. Schwab was impressed with Lee's confidence and told him to proceed.

Lee handed Schwab a piece of paper and said, "Write down the things you have to do tomorrow." Schwab did as he was instructed. "Now number these items in order of importance," Lee continued. Schwab did that. Then Lee gave Schwab his instructions. "First thing tomorrow morning, start working on #1 and stay with it until it is completed. Next take #2, and don't go any further until that is completed. Then proceed to #3, and so on. If you can't complete everything on the schedule, don't worry; at least you will have taken care of the most important things before getting distracted by the items of lesser consequence."

Lee said that if Schwab completed every item on the list before the day was done, he should make a new list and start on that; or, if any items were left at the end of the day, they could be considered for the next day's list. "The secret," Lee continued, "is to do this daily, evaluate the relative importance of the things you have to get done, establish your priorities, record your plan of action, and stick to it. Test it for as long as you like, teach your men, and then send me a check for whatever you think it is worth."

In a few weeks, Charles Schwab sent Ivy Lee a check for $25,000. This was big money in the 1930s. It was reported that Schwab told his associates that this was the single most valuable idea he had ever received.[80]

PUTTING IT ALL TOGETHER

The story of Bethlehem Steel and Charles Schwab reminds me that making a list is a good thing. *The Checklist Manifesto* is a book that extols the benefits of simple checklists. "We need a different strategy for overcoming failure, one that builds on experience and takes advantage of the knowledge people have but somehow also makes up for our inevitable human inadequacies. And there is such a strategy—though it will seem almost ridiculous in its simplicity, maybe even crazy to those of us who have spent years carefully developing ever more advanced skills and technologies. It is a checklist."[81] I currently use a daily planning system by Michael Hyatt that helps me create simple lists. These lists enable me to accomplish annual, quarterly, monthly, weekly, and daily goals. I've found checklists to be immensely helpful.

How would you like to narrow down the content in this book to something bite-sized and usable to bring health to your Sunday School?

Let's use simple lists to create a plan of action. The graphic below shows the process we'll go through.

First, you will identify your vision for your Sunday School. Next, you'll identify the most pressing needs you see. Third, you'll narrow those needs and create a priority list of the top three items you want to address. Then you'll determine the kind of improvement you're seeking. Finally, you'll write down action steps that will get you moving in the right direction.

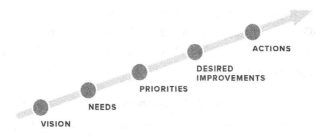

VISION

Imagine it's five years from now. Your church's Sunday School is healthier than it's ever been. Good things are taking place. What does that look like? What's going on? Articulate this improved status below, and craft a vision for your Sunday School: _____

_____

_____

_____

_____

NEEDS

There is a difference between the preferred future state of your Sunday School (see your vision statement above) and the way it is now.

As you think about your Sunday School's current state, based on your observations and learning from this book, what do you identify as the top five needs of your Sunday School? List those below:

1. _____

2. _____

3. _____

4. _____
5. _____

TOP PRIORITIES

After listing your Sunday School's five most pressing needs, force rank them and determine the top three priorities that will help your Sunday School experience increased health and vibrancy.

- Circle the top three priorities in your list above.
- Write #1, #2, and #3 to the left of the three items you circled. You will focus your energies and attention on these three things in the coming months.

DESIRED IMPROVEMENT

Now that you've identified your top three priorities, it's time to quantify them. In order to make them meaningful, you'll want to be specific in regard to the improvement you want to see.

For instance, don't say, "I want the Sunday School to grow" (although that is a good goal!). It is better to quantify the statement and express it like this: "I want the Sunday School of our church to grow by 20% over the next twelve months." This is specific, measurable, and realistic. If one of your goals is to start training group leaders, don't say, "I want to begin training group leaders." Instead, say, "I want to establish quarterly training for group leaders beginning January 1."

PRIORITY 1 _____

Desired Improvement _____

_____

PRIORITY 2 _____

Desired Improvement _____

_____

PRIORITY 3 _____

Desired Improvement _____

_____

ACTIONS

You're almost finished! You've pictured a desired future state in your Sunday School ministry. You've identified needs and prioritized them. You've also determined the improvements you want to see in the Sunday School. Now it is time to go one step further and list three actions you can take to work toward accomplishing each of your top three priorities.

PRIORITY 1
Action 1: _____
Action 2: _____
Action 3: _____

PRIORITY 2
Action 1: _____
Action 2: _____
Action 3: _____

PRIORITY 3
Action 1: _____
Action 2: _____
Action 3: _____

Filling out these lists will benefit your Sunday School for years to come as you act on them. As you accomplish your top three priorities, replace them with other priorities that didn't initially make your top three list. Keep chipping away at the things needed to improve your Sunday School and breathe new life into it.

CONCLUSION

Twelve essentials. Twelve principles any church can adopt to improve the health of its Sunday School ministry. These essentials are not hard to understand, nor are they difficult to implement. With prayer and planning, your Sunday School can make progress. It can regain its strength. It can be revived! It can have life breathed into it again.

Take small steps. But step. Keep moving forward. Remember a phrase that a friend of mine once told me: "A steady drop wears out the rock." Consistency is crucial when you want to bring about change. Be consistent in accomplishing the essentials suggested in this book. Stick to the basics. You'll see progress.

Vince Lombardi was famous for telling his players, "Gentlemen, this is a football." He held one up as he said those words. He made his players focus on the basics. To Lombardi, winning football games was all about blocking and tackling. To win championships, he believed a team had to execute the basics better than its opponent. He built his reputation and career on this belief. It turned out pretty good; he has a trophy named in his honor.[79]

Someone once said, "Sunday School isn't rocket science." Like football, it's about blocking and tackling—about doing the basics and executing them consistently. Sunday School works, but it's hard work.

The twelve essentials contained in this book will help you focus on blocking and tackling. That's what they are. The reason so many Sunday Schools are experiencing poor health today is because they've forgotten to do the basics with excellence. I pray that the twelve essentials will give you direction without being overly prescriptive. No one knows your church better than you do. Adjust these twelve essentials to fit your ministry context. Pray. Work hard. I believe God will bless your efforts, and your

Sunday School will become stronger and more vibrant.

At the beginning of the book I quoted Proverbs 21:31. It seems only fitting to conclude the book the same way. The Bible says, "A horse is prepared for the day of battle, but victory comes from the LORD" (Prov. 21:31). There's work to be done. There's effort to be expended. We must not be idle.

In the end, we are contending for the Lord's church. We are fighting for His people and for His name's sake. We are seeking to obey the Great Commission as we go about the important task of making disciples. The horse may be saddled, but always remember the victory belongs to the Lord.

It's time to saddle up. Are you ready to ride?

ENDNOTES

1   Vehicle Technologies Office, "Average Historical Annual Gasoline Pump Price, 1929-2015," accessed January 15, 2019, https://www.energy. gov/eere/vehicles/fact-915-march-7-2016-average-historical-annual-gasoline-pump-price-1929-2015.

2   "The Lord of the Rings: The Fellowship of the Ring," Warner Bros., accessed February 11, 2019, https://www.warnerbros.com/lord-rings-fellowship-ring.

3   "Wikipedia:About," Wikipedia, accessed February 11, 2019, https:// en.wikipedia.org/wiki/Wikipedia:About.

4   "US warship Reagan in service," BBC News, July 12, 2003, http://news. bbc.co.uk/2/hi/americas/3061865.stm.

5   David Francis, *Transformational Class* (Nashville: LifeWay Press, 2010), 21.

6   David Francis, *Missionary Sunday School* (Nashville: LifeWay Press, 2011), 18.

7   Rick Yount, *Created to Learn* (Nashville: B&H Academic, 2010), 560.

8   Howard G. Hendricks, *7 Laws of the Teacher,* (Peachtree Corners, GA: Walk Thru the Bible Ministries, 2011).

9   David Francis, Ken Braddy, Michael Kelley, *Teacher: Creating Conversational Community* (Nashville: LifeWay Press, 2015), 46–47.

10 Gary Newton, *Heart Deep Teaching* (Nashville: B&H Publishing, 2012), 109.

11 Howard Hendricks, *Teaching to Change Lives,* (Colorado Springs: Multnomah Books, 1987), 78.

12 John Milton Gregory, *The Seven Laws of Teaching,* (Eastford, CT: Martino

Fine Books, 2011), 32.

13 Carmine Gallo, *Talk Like TED: The 9 Public Speaking Secrets of the World's Top Minds* (New York: St. Martin's Griffin), 235.

14 Thomas A. Armstrong, *7 Kinds of Smart* (New York: Plume Publishing, 1994), 9.

15 Ibid., 9–11.

16 LeRoy Ford, *A Primer for Teachers and Leaders* (Nashville: The Sunday School Board of the Southern Baptist Convention, 1963), 139.

17 Brad Waggoner, *The Shape of Faith to Come* (Nashville: B&H Books, 2008), 68.

18 David Francis and Michael Kelley, *One Hundred: Charting a Course Past 100 in Sunday School* (Nashville: LifeWay Press, 2016), 38.

19 Allan Taylor, *The Six Core Values of Sunday School* (Canton, GA: Riverstone Group, 2003), 173.

20 Steve Parr, *Key Strategies for Healthy Sunday Schools* (Friendswood, TX: Baxter Press, 2008), 123.

21 Ed Stetzer and Mark Dodson, *Comeback Churches* (Nashville: B&H Books, 2007), 155-156.

22 Aubrey Malphurs and Will Mancini, *Building Leaders* (Grand Rapids: Baker Books, 2004), 27.

23 Research Services, Georgia Baptist Convention, February 2002.

24 Flake, Arthur, *Building a Standard Sunday School* (Nashville: The Sunday School Board of the Southern Baptist Convention, 1922), 124.

25 Steve Parr, *Key Strategies for Healthy Sunday Schools* (Friendswood, TX: Baxter Press, 2008), 61.

26 Wayne Poling, *Conducting Potential Sunday School Worker Training* (Nashville: Convention Press, 1992), 8.

27 George Barna, *The Frog in the Kettle* (Ventura, CA: Regal Books, 1990), 44.

28 Arthur Flake, *Building a Standard Sunday School* (Nashville: Sunday School Board of the Southern Baptist Convention, 1922), p.47.

29 David Francis, *Great Expectations* (Nashville: LifeWay Press, 2009), 40.

30 Ed Stetzer and Mike Dodson, *Comeback Churches* (Nashville: B&H Publishing Group, 2007), 157.

[31] David Francis, *Great Expectations* (Nashville: LifeWay Press, 2009), 12.

[32] Allan Taylor, *Sunday School in HD* (Nashville: B&H Books, 2009), 92.

[33] Merriam-Webster Online, "Myth," accessed February 11, 2019, https://www.merriam-webster.com/dictionary/myth.

[34] Andy Stanley, Reggie Joiner, and Lane Jones, *7 Practices of Effective Ministry* (New York: Crown Publishing Group, 2004), 73.

[35] Ibid., 71–75.

[36] Arthur Flake, *The True Functions of the Sunday School* (Nashville: Convention Press, 1955), 93.

[37] Ed Stetzer and Eric Geiger, *Transformational Groups* (Nashville: B&H Books, 2014), 33.

[38] Arthur Flake, *The True Functions of the Sunday School* (Nashville: The Sunday School Board of the Southern Baptist Convention, 1930), 17.

[39] Aubrey Malphurs, *Strategic Disciplemaking* (Grand Rapids: Baker Books, 2009) 33.

[40] Arthur Flake, *Building A Standard Sunday School* (Nashville: Sunday School Board of the Southern Baptist Convention, 1922), 98.

[41] Robby Gallaty, *Growing Up* (Nashville: B&H Publishing, 2013), 36.

[42] Jim Putman and Bobby Harrington with Robert E. Coleman, *DiscipleShift* (Grand Rapids: Zondervan, 2013), 171.

[43] David Francis and Rick Howerton, *Countdown* (Nashville: LifeWay Press, 2014), 30.

[44] Ed Stetzer and Eric Geiger, *Transformational Groups* (Nashville: B&H Books, 2014), 24.

[45] David Francis and Ken Braddy, *3 Roles for Guiding Groups*, (Nashville: LifeWay Press, 2013), 21–27

[46] Robby Gallaty, *Growing Up* (Nashville: B&H Publishing, 2013), 25.

[47] Eric Geiger and Thom Rainer, *Simple Church* (Nashville: B&H Publishing, 2006), 153.

[48] Allan Taylor, *Sunday School in HD* (Nashville: B&H Publishing, 2009), 37.

[49] Harry Piland, *Basic Sunday School Work* (Nashville: Convention Press, 1980), 125–129.

50 Baptist Press News, "Southern Baptist Sunday School Leader, Harry Piland, Dies," May 24, 2001, http://www.bpnews.net/10968/southern-baptist-sunday-school-leader-harry-piland-dies.

51 Steve Parr, *Key Strategies for Healthy Sunday Schools* (Houston: Baxter Press, 2008), 127.

52 Edward Ford, "Moneyball: How Big Data & Analytics Turned the Oakland A's into the Best Team in Baseball," The Sports Marketing Playbook, August 31, 2016, https://thesportsmarketingplaybook.com/2016/08/31/moneyball-how-big-data-analytics-turned-the-oakland-as-into-the-best-team-in-baseball/.

53 Kyle Jensen, "Red Sox: Boston's Recipe for Success," The Bleacher Report, April 10, 2008, https://bleacherreport.com/articles/17239-red-sox-bostons-recipe-for-success.

54 Ken Hemphill, *The Bonsai Theory of Church Growth* (Tigerville, SC: Auxano Press, 2011).

55 Bob Smietana, "Research: Unchurched Will Talk About Faith, Not Interested in Going to Church," LifeWay Research, June 28, 2016, https://lifewayresearch.com/2016/06/28/unchurched-will-talk-about-faith-not-interested-in-going-to-church/.

56 Chuck Lawless, *Membership Matters* (Grand Rapids: Zondervan, 2005), 95.

57 Thom S. Rainer, *High Expectations* (Nashville: B&H Books, 1999), 45.

58 Wayne Poling, *How to Sunday School Manual* (Nashville: LifeWay Press, 2009), 45.

59 Jerri Herring and Larry Garner, *5 Handles for Getting a Grip on your Sunday School* (Nashville: Jerri Herring and Larry Garner, 1997), 10.

60 Ibid.,10.

61 The Outreach Marketing Roadshow, Dallas, TX, 1996.

62 Thom Rainer, *Becoming a Welcoming Church* (Nashville: B & H Books, 2018), 9.

63 David Francis and Rick Howerton, *Countdown: Launching and Leading Transformational Groups* (Nashville: LifeWay Press, 2014), 38.

64 Arthur Flake, *Building a Standard Sunday School* (Nashville: Sunday School Board of the Southern Baptist Convention, 1922), 60.

65 Brad Waggoner, *The Shape of Faith to Come* (Nashville: B&H Books, 2008), 68.

66 David Francis and Michael Kelley, *One Hundred: Charting a Course Past 100 in Sunday school*, 24

67 "The Baptist Faith & Message." Sbc.net, Southern Baptist Convention, www.sbc.net/bfm/bfm2000.asp#ii

68 Eric Geiger and Ed Stetzer, *Transformational Groups* (Nashville: B&H Publishing, 2014), 57.

69 Eric Geiger and Ed Stetzer, *Transformational Groups* (Nashville: B&H Publishing, 2014), 57.

70 Robert Pazmino, *Foundational Issues in Christian Education* (Grand Rapids: Baker Academic, 2008), 147.

71 James Estep, Jr., Michael J. Anthony, and Gregg R. Allison, *A Theology for Christian Education* (Nashville: B&H Academic, 2014), 120.

72 Robert Pazmino, *Foundational Issues in Christian Education* (Grand Rapids: Baker Academic, 2008), 44.

73 James Estep, Jr., Michael J. Anthony, and Gregg R. Allison, *A Theology for Christian Education* (Nashville: B&H Academic, 2014), 162.

74 Ibid., 170.

75 Ibid., 170.

76 George R. Knight, *Philosophy & Education* (Berrien Springs, MI: Andrews University Press, 2006), 210.

77 James Estep, Jr., Michael J. Anthony, and Gregg R. Allison, *A Theology for Christian Education* (Nashville: B&H Academic, 2014), 171.

78 Robert Pazmino, *Foundational Issues in Christian Education* (Grand Rapids: Baker Academic, 2008), 140.

79 George R. Knight, *Philosophy & Education* (Berrien Springs, MI: Andrews University Press, 2006), 136.

80 Wayne Poling, The National Sunday School Director's Seminar, 2012

81 Atwul Gawande, *The Checklist Manifesto* (New York: Picador Publishing, 2009), 13.

Get everything you need for your next study
IN ONE BOX

Adults Group Box

When it's time to order resources for your next Bible study, just select one item: the *Adult Group Box*. It includes everything that each of your groups needs for a deep discipleship experience. And because the contents are part of an all-in-one package, you save more than 10 percent!

EACH ADULT GROUP BOX CONTAINS:
- 10 *Study Guides*
- 1 *Leader Guide**
- 1 *Leader Pack*
- Additional study helps
- Free Wordsearch Bible Digital Library
- 1 Quick Start Guide

Adults Group Box

Boxes are available for Bible Studies for Life, Explore the Bible, and The Gospel Project (* *Leader Guide* included in the *Daily Discipleship Guide* for this resource). Simply purchase one *Box* for each of your groups. (And order extra *Study Guides* for groups that have more than 10 people.)

Adults Group Box